sacred space

MEDITATIONS FOR COMMON PLACES

MATT WILL ✦ CHAP CLARK ✦ BEVERLY COOK
JIM HAMPTON ✦ KEVIN McGINNIS ✦ ED ROBINSON

ANCIENT FAITH SERIES

Barefoot Ministries®
Kansas City, Missouri

Copyright 2005
by Barefoot Ministries®

ISBN 083-415-0093

Printed in the
United States of America

Editor: Bo Cassell
Assistant Editor: Stephanie McNelly

Cover Design: Brandon Hill

Library of Congress Cataloging-in-Publication Data

Sacred space : meditations for common places / by Matt Will . . . [et al.].
    p. cm. — (Ancient faith series)
    Summary: "A guide to Christian station based prayer meditations of two types—those for everyday places such as a public park or campus, and those for use with a prayer path or labyrinth"—Provided by publisher.
    ISBN 0-8341-5009-3 (pbk.)
    1. Meditation—Christianity. 2. Prayer. 3. Meditations. 4. Sacred space. 5. Youth—Religious life.
I. Will, Matt (Matt Stephen), 1979- II. Title. III. Series.

    BV4813.S22 2005
    248.3—dc22

                                                              2005010987

10   9   8   7   6   5   4   3   2   1

Contents

PREFACE

This book is a handbook, a field guide to one of the ancient Christian disciplines, that of prayer journey meditation. It has the benefit of being usable in a traditional prayer path format, or in the everyday space we find ourselves in.

The whole design of this work is to answer a deep heart longing—the need to just get away and be with God. For those who hunger for that, they will find direction and help on their journey in the form of an ancient discipline that keeps distractions to a minimum.

It took the work of several authors to bring this book into reality. The first of which is Matt Will, a student working on his Masters in the Philippines. We are grateful to Matt for sending us a proposal, and letting us take it and run with it. In his experience at Simpson University in California and in his studies overseas, Matt has facilitated many prayer path experiences for college students and others. We have drawn from the depth of his knowledge and experience to bring you this work. We are likewise grateful for the contributions of three Seminary professors of Christian Education and Youth Ministry: Dr. Chap Clark, Associate Professor of Youth, Family and Culture at Fuller Theological Seminary; Jim Hampton (soon to be Dr.), Assistant Professor of Youth Ministry at Asbury Theological Seminary; and Dr. Ed Robinson, longtime seminary professor and now president of MidAmerica Nazarene University. We are grateful that these busy men took the time to contribute to this project. In addition, we gratefully acknowledge the contributions of two long time Youth Pastors, Beverly Cook and Kevin McGinnis. Between them they have dozens of years of experience working with teens and young adults. All of these authors bring tremendous insight to these meditations—which comes from their shared heart to see youth and college students deepen their walk with Christ. Thank you one and all.

We trust that this work will assist those who long to turn everyday space into sacred space.

Bo Cassell
Barefoot Ministries® Editor

How to Use This Book

God's creation is sacred because God has touched it. And because you are God's creation, you are sacred too. Just like the burning bush, where God is present that space is holy—it is sacred ground. When we draw close to God, we meet Him in sacred space. God turns our everyday lives into something sacramental and holy—God turns our everyday space into sacred space.

Sacred Space: Meditations for Common Places is your guide to an ancient practice for drawing closer to God. It involves prayer and meditation using prayer journeys. A prayer journey is a meditation that is done by moving through different stations, concentrating on a different aspect of the meditation at each station. The unique thing about this book is that it takes this ancient Christian practice and brings it into everyday life and everyday space. It provides meditations that youth and young adults can use in places right in the world where they live—the park, their campus, any outdoor setting—everyday spaces. In addition, there are several "traditional" meditations that can be done on a prayer path or just about anywhere. If you are interested in creating a prayer path for a group or event, some hints are provided here as well. To help you quickly understand what you have in your hands, here is a quick description of this book and a simple outline of how to use it.

A Description and Summary of *Sacred Space:*

- *Sacred Space* is a book of "station based" prayer journey meditations for people who hunger to draw closer to Christ.
- A prayer journey is a discipline to help you draw closer to God and get rid of distractions. When you do this kind of meditation, you are active—you physically move from station to station, using a different prayer focus at each one to guide you.
- There are two kinds of meditations in this book—those designed for a particular "space" (a park, the mall, etc.) and traditional meditations. The traditional meditations are generally used on a prayer path or prayer labyrinth, but they can be used just about anywhere. The idea is to be able to take this book and go

for a walk with God, meeting Him in a common, everyday place—and then seeing that place in a whole new way because you meet with God there.

- For those who are interested in the ancient practice of walking a prayer path, some helps on how to get started are included. A prayer path experience for personal use or for groups and events can be easily facilitated with several copies of this book and a few simple materials. (For a free step-by-step guide to setting up a prayer path, and facilitator's guidelines, visit www.barefootministries.com!)

How to Use This Book—Quick and Simple:

- Select a meditation from the table of contents and (if appropriate) decide on a location where you will walk through the meditation.
- Open up to the meditation and begin to read. Start at "Station 1," read the explanation and follow any *Action* steps.
- Read any of the *Scripture Reading Options* that you wish. We have provided the first Scripture or two to get started. You can also take out a Bible and look up the "Go Deeper" Options for additional Scriptures to study that are appropriate to that meditation. Read the Scripture several times slowly. Take time to focus your thoughts and prayerfully receive what it says. Read slowly and take your time to reflect on what God is saying to you through the Scriptures.
- Pray through any of the *Prayer Options* or a prayer of your own. Take your time, relax, and enjoy your time with God.
- When you are finished with that station, get up and walk to another location for "Station 2." Move to another location slowly and prayerfully. The "journeys" in between stations are part of the process! The movement represents your life journey with God, and the new setting will help you to see things in new ways.
- As you work through "Meditations for Common Places," you will be directed to find specific locations. Some of them may not correspond exactly to where you live. Don't be afraid to improvise and use your imagination! They need not be exact. Skip a station if necessary. The important thing is to spend time with God. When you work through a "Traditional Meditation," you

can walk a prayer path "labyrinth," or just invent your own path wherever you are! Just pick several landmarks and move from one to another for your stations.

- You can really do these meditations anytime, anywhere! Just select a meditation, start by walking to any space, object, or landmark, and begin reading the meditations for "Station 1." When you are finished with that station, look up, and select another landmark, and prayerfully move to that location and read the material for "Station 2." Work your way through as many stations as you wish, taking as much time as you need at each station. Relax and "take a walk with God."

- Do these steps through as many of the stations as are helpful to you to draw close to God.

Use the meditations in this book as a means of drawing closer to the Lord. You can use this book for your personal use or together with others. Allow Christ to use the prayer journey and the Scriptures to form who He has made you to be. Allow yourself to rest. Take the time truly to live as you reflect on what the Lord is doing in your life.

SACRED SPACE:
AN INTRODUCTION TO THE PRAYER JOURNEY

We rarely stop to realize that we are alive. As we go from one moment to the next, we jump from one event on our calendar to another, never stopping to realize that we have the breath of life within our
bodies. Our pace is so hectic, that we feel like we are living a worn-
out life. We get so involved in running our lives that we forget to live.
In *Space for God,* Don Postema quotes the character Emily from the
Thorton Wilder's play *Our Town:* "Do any human beings ever realize
life while they live it—every, every minute?"[1] Think about it—how often
do we stop to listen to our breath or put our hand on our chest to
feel our heartbeat? These are good questions to ask as we stop and
reflect using the prayer journey meditations found in this book. These
kind of meditations have the profound ability to help us stop and *realize* life as we live it. Do you realize life as you live it? Or are you too
caught up with school and meetings to realize life as you are living it?

Life is a prayer journey. We enter this life and realize that, to be
formed and changed, we must stop often in our journey and spend
time before God our Maker. We must pause and take the time to
grab hold of the authenticity of His love. Many different disciplines
can help us on our journey. It is our hope that this book will provide
tools to help you spend time with your Maker in a new way. *Sacred
Space* is one more tool to facilitate encountering Christ in everyday
moments and in everyday places. We hope that through these meditations, you will begin to look at the common places you inhabit
every day with new eyes—that you would see your life differently—and
that you would see God in a new way.

Prayer Journey Meditations?

So what are these meditations, or "prayer journey meditations" as
we sometimes like to call them? Meditation is concentrating all your

---

1. Don Postema, *Space for God: Study and Practice of Spirituality and Prayer* (Grand Rapids, Michigan:
Faith Alive, 1997), 16.

thoughts on something, or sort of praying and thinking about something at the same time. When we meditate, we pray and think and listen—we give God the chance to speak to us. The unique thing about the meditations in this book is that they are "prayer journey" meditations. They are meditations you do in motion—as you move from one place to another. You pray as you journey, focusing your attention on a particular Scripture and thought at each stopping point along the way. Think of it as taking a walk with God. It is an active way to turn your attention to Him.

Why Pray This Way?

Currently there is a hunger for authenticity and a desire to embrace the mystery of life. As you read this, ask yourself if you have hungered for authenticity and the mystery of God. This ancient tool allows the journeyer to have both. These kind of meditations seek *formational* reading of the Scripture (reading to be changed), not *informational* reading. Journeyers are challenged to step into a "sacred space" and be received and accepted by their Heavenly Father.

The prayer journey can lend itself to many spiritual metaphors. It is a visual tool representing the reality that we are on a journey in our Christian walk. Just as a prayer path winds closer to and further from the center, at times we will feel closer to Christ and at times we feel further away. Still, the journey remains constant. On this journey, what we learn and how we change are what matters, not just the destination.

In Community

This book is designed so that an individual can pick it up and begin to use it on his or her own. However, we would like to encourage you to use it with a partner or in groups. God has designed us to be in community, and there is much to be gained from practicing meditation with others. Although the prayer journey appears to be a very private discipline, it is at the same time a communal practice. We are all individuals on a journey growing closer to God. Yet at the same time, we are unified in that we are all walking the same path. The Holy Spirit unifies us as we journey in the same direction. We may deal with individual hurts and joys, but we are also being formed to help one another and grow together.

section one

MEDITATIONS FOR COMMON PLACES

MEDITATION FOR A PUBLIC PARK

BY KEVIN McGINNIS

Every public park is different, but they all serve one purpose—recreation. For this meditation, you will select different elements that are common to most parks, and they will serve as your stopping points for meditation and prayer. Don't worry if one of the elements is missing—simply use your imagination and improvise or substitute, or just skip to the next station.

The goal of this set of meditations is to turn this space designed for recreation into sacred space designed for re-creation. By reminding ourselves of God's presence, we see fields of grass, swing sets, water, and other elements as the tools God uses to re-create His image in us and remind us that we are His.

If at all possible, find a park that has a pond, lake, or pool. You may wish to bring your Bible, some blank paper, a pen, and some sort of towel or blanket as well.

 ## STATION I—BEGINNINGS: REMOVING DISTRACTIONS

We want the Holy Spirit to lead us through this prayer path. Sometimes the first step to hearing God's Spirit speak to us is to shut out all the other voices that seek our attention. Begin your time in the park by shutting out distractions and slowing down enough to give your soul a chance to catch up with your body.

ACTION: *Take a moment and look for the most relaxing and highest spot in the park, a place that can give you a good view of the area* *(even if that is a bench or a table). Sit down and relax. Get comfortable. Spend the next few minutes here.*

Take out a blank piece of paper. Write down everything that is racing through your head that could be a distraction to you during the path. Wad it all up into a ball. While holding your new paper ball, take the next few moments to meditate on a scripture from "Scripture Reading Options." Allow every distraction between you and God to become quiet. Find the nearest trash can and throw away your paper ball—if any distractions come back to your mind, remind yourself that you have thrown those away for now, and turn your attention back to God.

Scripture Reading Options

PSALM 46:10

Be still, and know that I am God.

PSALM 86:11

Teach me your way, O LORD, and I will walk in your truth; give me an undivided heart, that I may fear your name.

GO DEEPER—ROMANS 12:1-8

Prayer Options

PRAYER OPTION 1:

Lord Jesus, I pray that Your Holy Spirit would meet me here. Take these distractions and quiet them. I am here waiting to hear from You. Grant me peace as I journey with You. Amen.

PRAYER OPTION 2:

(Take time to pray over your list of things that are on your mind. One by one, give them to God, and as you hand them to God in your prayer, say "Lord I trust You to handle this for the next hour so that I may worship You.")

Key/Memory Verse

HEBREWS 12:1-2

Therefore, since we are surrounded by such a great cloud of witnesses, let us throw off everything that hinders and the sin that so easily entangles, and let us run with perseverance the race marked out for us. Let us fix our eyes on Jesus, the author and perfecter of our faith, who for the joy set before him endured the cross, scorning its shame, and sat down at the right hand of the throne of God.

 ## STATION 2—PATHS

Some paths are put in place on purpose—they are paved with gravel, stones, or just intentionally marked in the dirt. Some paths are formed accidentally because enough people who were going the same direction wear the ground until a path is formed. Some paths are unmarked. We find our way as we go. The path becomes our symbol for our journey through life. For this meditation, we are going to walk a path of praise, and enjoy our Maker and His creation.

ACTION: *Find the best path that will take you through the center of the park, if possible. (If there is not a designated path, create your own! Just find your way as you go.) Walk the path you have chosen around the park. Take your time. Let your senses take in God's creation—the trees, birds, grass, rocks, and sky—everything He has made. Think of words that describe our Creator as well as other names of praise attributed to Him. Try to think of as many as you can while you walk slowly, observing what He has made. When you have a list of names of praise, stop and write them down, or select one to keep in mind as you walk. Worship the Lord by giving Him praise for His wonderful works.*

Scripture Reading Options

PSALM 145:1-4

I will exalt you, my God the King; I will praise your name for ever and ever. Every day I will praise you and extol your name for ever and ever. Great is the LORD and most worthy of praise; his greatness no one can fathom. One generation will commend your works to another; they will tell of your mighty acts.

PSALM 145:6-9

They will tell of the power of your awesome works, and I will proclaim your great deeds. They will celebrate your abundant goodness and joyfully sing of your righteousness. The LORD is gracious and compassionate, slow to anger and rich in love. The LORD is good to all; he has compassion on all he has made.

GO DEEPER—PSALM 145:1-21

Prayer Options

PRAYER OPTION 1:

My Father in heaven, praise Your holy name! You are wonderful. Your creation displays the loving care You have for us. I just wanted You to know I love You for who You are, and not just for what You have done for me. Amen.

PRAYER OPTION 2:

God, no matter where my paths may wind, I will praise You. No matter where I go, You are with me, and I will give You thanks. Even when I stray from Your ways, You gently guide me back to the good paths—I praise You for Your compassionate heart. Your creation is all around me, Your love surrounds me, I can see Your wonderful works everywhere I go. God of all creation, may Your name be praised.

Key/Memory Verse

PSALM 145:5

They will speak of the glorious splendor of your majesty, and I will meditate on your wonderful works.

 STATION 3—BOUNDARIES

"God is a killjoy; He doesn't want you to have any fun. The more boring your life, the happier God is. Everything that is fun, God made off-limits." If we were honest with ourselves, most of us would admit we have had thoughts like these.

The truth is that the boundaries and limits God has set before us have a good purpose—to keep us from harm. A good father sets limits for his children to protect them. We can be thankful for a God who has created boundaries for us.

ACTION: *Move to a fence that separates one area from another, or a sidewalk that separates the park from the street. Walk along this barrier. Consider why the barrier was put there. Why does it exist? Is it for safety? What would happen if it wasn't there? Next, begin walking around the perimeter of the park. Make a note of all of the rules you see posted. (For example: "No glass containers," "Throw away your trash," etc.) Think for a moment of some of the rules of the park that are not* *posted. Then think about your life. What God-given boundaries have been protecting your heart, your future, and your body? Why do you think God made those rules and laws? What would happen if they weren't there? Sit for a moment by one of these boundaries and humbly talk to God about the boundaries He has put around your life to guard you. Give thanks to God for caring enough to protect you.*

Scripture Reading Options

PSALM 1:2-3

But his delight is in the law of the LORD, and on his law he meditates day and night. He is like a tree planted by streams of water, which yields its fruit in season and whose leaf does not wither. Whatever he does prospers.

PSALM 119:23-24

Though rulers sit together and slander me, your servant will meditate on your decrees. Your statutes are my delight; they are my counselors.

GO DEEPER—PROVERBS 2:1-22

Prayer Options

PRAYER OPTION 1:

Dear Heavenly Father, thank You for boundaries. Thank You for knowing what is best for me. I thank You for Your Word. Help me as I hide it in my heart, so that I might not sin and that I may live for You. Amen.

PRAYER OPTION 2:

Lord, thank You for loving me so much. I appreciate the boundaries You have set for me. Give me discernment to recognize lies that would trap me. Help me as I pursue the truth and live by Your Spirit. Keep me from trying to "walk the fence," with one foot standing on Your truth and another in a place of danger. Protect me from crossing lines that would place me in harm's way. I seek to look to You and follow only Your ways.

Key/Memory Verse

PSALM 119:23-24

Though rulers sit together and slander me, your servant will meditate on your decrees. Your statutes are my delight; they are my counselors.

STATION 4—ATHLETIC FIELD

Sports are a big part of recreation. They are a fun way to challenge ourselves to do better. Sometimes we can get overwhelmed by competition and become consumed by it. But if we can lay aside the competition, athletics can help us grow and inspire us to be the best we can be.

ACTION: *Walk (or if you wish, run) to an athletic field—soccer field, baseball diamond, basketball court—or even to a group of people throwing a Frisbee. Walk around the area, and think through the rules for that sport. Stop for a moment to consider all of the training that goes into a sport. Prayerfully reflect on how in athletics, people push each other toward excellence in pursuit of a common goal. Also remember the cutting edge of competition—when we become too obsessed with it, we stop treating others with love.*

Spend some time with the Lord evaluating your commitment to training to excel in your spiritual life. In prayer, talk to God about your willingness to play by the rules and pursue a common goal with your Heavenly Father.

Scripture Reading Options

2 TIMOTHY 2:5

Similarly, if anyone competes as an athlete, he does not receive the victor's crown unless he competes according to the rules.

2 TIMOTHY 4:7-8

I have fought the good fight, I have finished the race, I have kept the faith. Now there is in store for me the crown of righteousness, which the Lord, the righteous Judge, will award to me on that day—and not only to me, but also to all who have longed for his appearing.

GO DEEPER—HEBREWS 12:1-13; I CORINTHIANS 9:24-27

Prayer Options

PRAYER OPTION I:

Lord, I realize that there are many days that I do not push myself to excellence for Your kingdom. I run toward You at a pace I know I am comfortable with—I do not challenge myself. I know there are many days that I don't run this race to win. Forgive me, Father. Give me the heart of a true athlete—a spiritual athlete—that I may run to win. Amen.

PRAYER OPTION 2:

Lord Jesus, have mercy on me when I make competition an end in itself. Forgive me when I compare myself to others, instead of seeing myself as You see me. Give me a spirit of love for myself—that I may push myself to excellence without comparison. Give me a spirit of love for others, that I may see this spiritual race as a team effort, and so I may not leave my brothers and sisters behind, but carry them when they are weak. Give me a humble heart that I may receive their support when I need to be carried. Amen.

Key/Memory Verse

I TIMOTHY 4:8

For physical training is of some value, but godliness has value for all things, holding promise for both the present life and the life to come.

 STATION 5—WATER

We can't live without water. It is one of the most basic elements of life. Water is a vivid symbol in everyday life—it refreshes and cleanses. It reminds us of our baptism—immersing our life into the faith, burying the old life and rising to the new, Spirit-soaked life.

Jesus spoke of living water that would never run dry. We can have a life that springs up from His Spirit within us and overflows into every area of our life. And the best part is that this living water never runs dry—it eternally quenches our thirst.

ACTION: *If there is one located in this park, walk to a pond, waterfall, pool, or a drinking fountain—some place where you can see water. Find a place to sit nearby. Get close to the water. If you can, touch the water, reaching out to feel it on your hands. If you have some water to drink, take a good, long, cool drink. (If you have been baptized, spend some time remembering back to that moment.)*

Reflect on the image of water, and talk to God about your greatest need that His living water can fulfill—do you need to be cleansed? Refreshed? Are you longing to have your thirst for God satisfied? Tell God about your need, and finish your time by affirming that you need God like you need water—without Him you cannot survive. If you can, as you leave this station, touch the water with your hand, and then touch it to your forehead. As you do this pray a one sentence prayer, something like, "Lord, I need Your living water today." This is a physical gesture that serves to remind us of our daily need for Him.

Scripture Reading Options

PSALM 42:1-2

As the deer pants for streams of water, so my soul pants for you, O God. My soul thirsts for God, for the living God. When can I go and meet with God?

EZEKIEL 36:25

I will sprinkle clean water on you, and you will be clean; I will cleanse you from all your impurities and from all your idols.

MARK 1:9-11

At that time Jesus came from Nazareth in Galilee and was baptized by John in the Jordan. As Jesus was coming up out of the water, he saw heaven being torn open and the Spirit descending on him like a dove. And a voice came from heaven: "You are my Son, whom I love; with you I am well pleased."

GO DEEPER—JOHN 4:1-14

Prayer Options

PRAYER OPTION 1:

Dear Lord Jesus, thank You for Your promise of eternal life. Fill me with Your living water. I pray that You would refresh my spirit today. Send Your life-giving Spirit like rain. I need Your touch—I need to drink from Your life-giving fountain. Fill me, Lord. Amen.

PRAYER OPTION 2:

Lord Jesus, I need to be cleansed today. My heart is dirty from the world, from my sin, and I need You to wash me today with Your cleansing water. Make me pure and clean by the power of Your Spirit. Take away my grime and guilt, and fill me with Your pure cleansing water. Amen.

Key/Memory Verse

HEBREWS 10:22

Let us draw near to God with a sincere heart in full assurance of faith, hav-

ing our hearts sprinkled to cleanse us from a guilty conscience and having our bodies washed with pure water.

 ## STATION 6—SHADE

Shade blocks us from the hot harsh rays of the sun. It is a place where we can cool down and rest from working or playing. Shade means cover, protection, and rest.

ACTION: *Go to a comfortable shady place, under a tree or next to a wall and sit down. Practice finding rest in God. Relax, close your eyes, and talk to God. If you fall asleep, that's OK. In fact, if you can lay down, or bow your head and close your eyes, that is good too. Allow your body to slow down, and even drift off to sleep. Let Jesus be the last thing on your mind before you drift off to rest. If you brought a picnic blanket or a beach towel, find a nice shady spot to lie down for a while. Just rest in the comfort of the shade, and pray as you feel led. Reflect on the fact that God knows you and knows you need rest. Take a break from the heat of the sun, and the fast pace of life, slow down and just rest. If you fall asleep, give thanks to God as soon as you wake up for the rest He provides.*

Scripture Reading Options

PSALM 121:5

The LORD watches over you—the LORD is your shade at your right hand.

ISAIAH 25:4

You have been a refuge for the poor, a refuge for the needy in his distress, a shelter from the storm and a shade from the heat.

MATTHEW 11:28

Come to me, all you who are weary and burdened, and I will give you rest.

GO DEEPER—1 KINGS 19:3-7

Prayer Options

PRAYER OPTION 1:

Lord, when Elijah was tired and weak, fleeing from evil people, he found shade under a tree. You provided for him when he was afraid and tired. Life looked so dark that he wanted to quit and just die. But

You provided rest for the spiritual battle he was fighting. Lord, I need Your shade, I need Your strength. Come and give me Your rest.

PRAYER OPTION 2:

(Repeat one of the short verses from "Scripture Reading Options" for this station. Repeat it several times, slowly and prayerfully.)

Key/Memory Verse

PSALM 121:5

The LORD watches over you—the LORD is your shade at your right hand.

 ## STATION 7—PLAY

Just about every animal on the planet plays. God has built fun into us. Sometimes we forget this and we turn the Christian life into a serious, robotic exercise. But God has made us to enjoy life and the creation He has given us. If we don't play, we become something less than human.

When we play, we are open to taking some risks. Climb to the top of the monkey bars. Jump from the highest diving board. Swing as high as you can on the swing set! This small element of risk reminds us that we are alive. For a little while, we forget about all the cares and burdens we carry. The schoolwork, the chores, our troubles . . . we need to remember that God is there with us all along, and we don't need to be overwhelmed with the cares of life. God is with us, He loves us, and He has given us life—it is OK to enjoy it!

ACTION: *Make your way to a children's playground, a swing set, or just find a group of people or children at play. Try to remember the last time you rode on a swing, went down a slide, or climbed the monkey bars. Then, go ahead! Play!*

Take a few minutes to play on the playground. Set this book down and go play on your favorite play equipment. Release your cares for the moment and allow God to see His child at play. (If there is not a place to play, walk around the park and sing to yourself and to God.)

Scripture Reading Options

PSALM 51:8

Let me hear joy and gladness; let the bones you have crushed rejoice.

MEDITATION FOR A PUBLIC PARK

I Samuel 16:23

Whenever the spirit from God came upon Saul, David would take his harp and play. Then relief would come to Saul; he would feel better, and the evil spirit would leave him.

2 Samuel 6:14

David, wearing a linen ephod, danced before the LORD with all his might.

Go Deeper—Leviticus 23:39-40

Prayer Options

Prayer Option 1:

Lord, thank You for opportunities to play. Show me ways that I can spend more time with You in Your presence. Speak to my heart and direct my mind to the places where I need to take some healthy risks for You. Grant me courage and wisdom and give me a sense of peace. Help me to keep my life balanced, Lord.

Key/Memory Verse

Psalm 96:11-12

Let the heavens rejoice, let the earth be glad; let the sea resound, and all that is in it; let the fields be jubilant, and everything in them. Then all the trees of the forest will sing for joy.

 ## STATION 8—RENEWED PRIORITIES

When we break our routine, and move from work, school, or home space to a re-creative space like a park, it gives us a new perspective on our daily world. By taking a deep breath in a park, we can get a whole new outlook on life and work. As we near the end of this meditation, take a few moments to walk and talk with God about the "space" where you will return to live.

ACTION: *Find a high point in the park where you can overlook as much of the park as possible (a hilltop, the top of some playground equipment, etc.) Take a moment to take in the view, and think about the difference between your view and God's view.*

Find a place to sit and recall some of the "distractions" you wrote down at Station 1, or review some of your current burdens and respon-sibilities. Bring them before the Lord and ask Him to help you rearrange the priorities of your life. Ask God to help you see all the areas of your life from His perspective. Bring Him any cares or concerns you have, and ask Him to help you handle them. Don't forget to include time with God as one of your top priorities.

Scripture Reading Options

Psalm 25:4

Show me your ways, O Lord, teach me your paths.

Proverbs 21:2

All a man's ways seem right to him, but the Lord weighs the heart.

Go Deeper—Matthew 6:25-33

Prayer Options

Prayer Option 1:

Lord, help me to order my life according to Your priorities. I take my life, and all responsibilities, and lay them at Your feet. Please take them, rearrange them, and turn them into something wonderful for Your kingdom.

Prayer Option 2:

Lord, let me see with new eyes. Unstop my ears that I may hear You, open my eyes that I may see You, renew my heart that I may know You. I pray that You would give me the grace to see life differ-ently. Don't let me get caught up in the spin of the world. Put my feet on solid ground, and give me peace. Amen.

Key/Memory Verse

Matthew 6:33

But seek first his kingdom and his righteousness, and all these things will be given to you as well.

 ## STATION 9—THE JOURNEY TO COME

We're coming to the end of our prayer path. Spend these last minutes reflecting on where you've been and what you have seen. How did God speak to you today? What have you trusted Him with? How have your plans changed?

ACTION: *Head to the place you began your journey today (Station 1). Before you head back to the business of life, take time to commit your way to God. Use the Lord's Prayer as your closing prayer.*

Pick up a small stone to carry with you this week. Use it as a reminder of your experience here. Leave it in your pocket, and whenever you notice it, say a short prayer of thanksgiving and praise to Jesus that He has been and always will be with you.

Scripture Reading Options

MATTHEW 6:9-13

In this manner, therefore, pray:

> *Our Father in heaven,*
> *Hallowed be Your name.*
> *Your kingdom come.*
> *Your will be done*
> *On earth as it is in heaven.*
> *Give us this day our daily bread.*
> *And forgive us our debts,*
> *As we forgive our debtors.*
> *And do not lead us into temptation,*
> *But deliver us from the evil one.*
> *For Yours is the kingdom and the power and the glory forever. Amen.*
> (NKJV)

JEREMIAH 29:11

"For I know the plans I have for you," declares the LORD, "plans to prosper you and not to harm you, plans to give you hope and a future."

Prayer Options

PRAYER OPTION 1:

(Say aloud the Lord's Prayer from Matthew 6:9-13, above.)

PRAYER OPTION 2:

Lord, thank You for taking a walk with me today in Your creation. I thank You for renewing me, refreshing me, and giving me peace. I love You, Lord. Amen.

Key/Memory Verse

PROVERBS 3:5-6

Trust in the LORD with all your heart and lean not on your own understanding; in all your ways acknowledge him, and he will make your paths straight.

MEDITATION FOR THE MALL

BY BEVERLY COOK

The mall is a great place for shopping and hanging out—but meditation? Malls have become a symbol of materialism, consumerism, and convenience. They contain everything from health food stores to the junk food court and from costume jewelry to expensive diamonds.

In this land of misplaced values (they put many stores in one place for convenience, but long walks and difficult parking make them somewhat inconvenient), we look to see what God would teach us.

In this sacred space, you get the chance to see the mall, and the people in it, through completely different eyes. In this meditation, you will work through one section of Scripture, the Sermon on the Mount, found in Matthew 5—7. We've chosen this section of Scripture because in it Jesus describes Kingdom values, which we will compare and contrast to the world's values as we find them in the mall. As you prepare for this particular prayer path, begin asking God to transform the way you live out His Kingdom principles in our materialistic world.

 ## STATION I—THE ENTRANCE

As we enter into this world, we stop to focus our eyes on those who enter with us. Before we spend time with God in this setting, we take time to humble our hearts and realize that we don't always see other people (or ourselves) with the eyes of God. We must remember that as we look at others, we must also take a close look at ourselves in order to keep a proper perspective.

sacred space

ACTION: *Pick any entrance to the mall, preferably a well used one. Sit down and watch people go by for five minutes or so. Make a mental list of the different types of people you see. Consider some of these categories:*

People of different races	*Clothing Styles*
Types of families	*Handicapped or Disabled*
Ages	*Income Level*
Hairstyles	

Reflect for a moment on how we see people—and how God sees them. Try to imagine the life story of some of the people who pass through the door. Who are they and how do they see themselves? How do you see them? As you read and reflect, try to imagine how God sees them.

Scripture Reading Options

I SAMUEL 16:7

But the LORD said to Samuel, "Do not consider his appearance or his height, for I have rejected him. The LORD does not look at the things man looks at. Man looks at the outward appearance, but the LORD looks at the heart."

MATTHEW 7:3-5

Why do you look at the speck of sawdust in your brother's eye and pay no attention to the plank in your own eye? How can you say to your brother, "Let me take the speck out of your eye," when all the time there is a plank in your own eye? You hypocrite, first take the plank out of your own eye, and then you will see clearly to remove the speck from your brother's eye.

GO DEEPER—MATTHEW 5:3-12

Prayer Options

PRAYER OPTION I:

(Reflect on what God was saying to you through the scripture. Then, pray this for yourself, filling in the blanks with a word or phrase that fits where you are right now.)

"Lord, when people look at me, they see _____.
But on the inside, what they fail to see is _____.
What I need most from You right now is _____.
Bring me Your _____. Amen."

PRAYER OPTION 2:

Lord Jesus, without a doubt, there are people who just walked by me that are hurting. Please comfort them. There are those attempting to be kind to their mom or dad or spouse but are still being rejected. Show them Your kindness today. For those who feel like the world is beating up on them, grant them the keys of Your Kingdom this very moment. Jesus, some are seeking to bring peace into a broken family or relationship. Allow them to hear Your words of acceptance today. It's a hurting world, Lord. We try to look like we have it all together. Beyond the right clothes and bright smile, however, is pain, fear, and insecurity. Be near to those in particular need of the Almighty God, Lord. Today Lord, be near to them. Amen.

Key/Memory Verse

I SAMUEL 16:7

The LORD does not look at the things man looks at. Man looks at the out-ward appearance, but the LORD looks at the heart.

 ## STATION 2—A CANDLE STORE

In the midst of a hurting world, we are called to be a light, leading the way to Christ. Our role in this world is to bring flavor to blandness, light to darkness. Standing up for Christ on a high school or college campus is one of the most difficult challenges we are called to face. But it becomes much easier when we are on fire with a passion to live for God.

ACTION: *Find a candle store, or a stationery store that has candles. As you wander through the store, pick up several different candles and smell their aroma. Explore the candles, and find a scent you like. As you do, think of ways your can light your world for Christ. See if you can find a candle that reminds you of a friend or person you know who does not know Jesus. Take time to pray specifically for a friend who needs Christ. (If you wish, you can purchase that candle and light it to remind yourself to pray for your friend.) Leave the store to finish your reading and prayer for this station.*

Scripture Reading Options

MATTHEW 5:13-16

You are the salt of the earth. But if the salt loses its saltiness, how can it be made salty again? It is no longer good for anything, except to be thrown out and trampled by men.

You are the light of the world. A city on a hill cannot be hidden. Neither do people light a lamp and put it under a bowl. Instead they put it on its stand, and it gives light to everyone in the house. In the same way, let your light shine before men, that they may see your good deeds and praise your Father in heaven.

ISAIAH 42:6

I, the LORD, have called you in righteousness; I will take hold of your hand. I will keep you and will make you to be a covenant for the people and a light for the Gentiles.

GO DEEPER—MATTHEW 5:17-26

Prayer Options

PRAYER OPTION 1:

Father, the way we live out our faith is like a candle—I pray that my light would burn bright, that there would be no question as to where my allegiance lies—my life is Yours. I pray my life would be filled with the sweet aroma of Your Spirit. Wherever I go, may I bring light and peace because You are with me.

PRAYER OPTION 2:

Lord, I pray for my friends. I pray for those I know who do not know You. I pray that You would fill me with Your light—that the light of Christ would be bright in me. Fill me with Your Spirit so that my friends might see You in me. Amen.

Key/Memory Verse

MATTHEW 7:8

For everyone who asks receives; he who seeks finds; and to him who knocks, the door will be opened.

 ## STATION 3—AN EXPENSIVE JEWELRY STORE

Jewelry is beautiful, sparkling, and enjoyable. We appreciate it for fashion and for status. But when all is said and done, it is nothing more than some metal and stones from the ground. We attach high price tags because of their sparkle value, but they are nothing more than rocks and ore from the dirt. The same goes for money—it is melted metals formed into round discs and paper and ink. In a very real sense, they are nothing more. Yet our culture prizes these things so much that we will do almost anything to get them. We treat people who have riches differently than those who don't have them.

ACTION: *Spend a moment browsing through the jewelry store. Pick out your favorite item, a watch, a ring, or a necklace. A store employee will probably ask if you need help. Note how they treat you if they find out you are "just looking" and not buying. Make note of the price of some of the items. Leave the store and find a place to sit down to read and pray.*

Scripture Reading Options

MATTHEW 6:19-21

Do not store up for yourselves treasures on earth, where moth and rust destroy, and where thieves break in and steal. But store up for yourselves treasures in heaven, where moth and rust do not destroy, and where thieves do not break in and steal. For where your treasure is, there your heart will be also.

MATTHEW 6:22-23

The eye is the lamp of the body. If your eyes are good, your whole body will be full of light. But if your eyes are bad, your whole body will be full of darkness. If then the light within you is darkness, how great is that darkness!

GO DEEPER—LUKE 12:16-21

Prayer Options

PRAYER OPTION 1:

Lord, I can see that the values of this world do not match the values of Your Kingdom. If my eyes crave the treasures of this world, my whole life will be upside-down. If I let myself get caught up in all the treasures this world has to offer, I will miss all things that You have to offer. Lord God, keep my eyes on You. Don't let me lose sight of You. Make me blind to the sparkle of the world. Amen.

PRAYER OPTION 2:

(Reflect for a moment on the value of the treasures of this world. Imagine what it would be like to visit the same jewelry store if you were blind. Would you pay the same price for the jewelry? Spend some time before God evaluating your values and the values of your culture.)

Key/Memory Verse

MATTHEW 6:24

No one can serve two masters. Either he will hate the one and love the other, or he will be devoted to the one and despise the other. You cannot serve both God and Money.

 ## STATION 4—STORE WINDOW

Every store puts sale signs, mannequins, and pictures in their window to draw people to enter and spend money. You have probably heard the phrase, "sex sells." Very often stores will exploit the human image to try to capture the attention of those passing by. The constant assault of images affects the thought life of men and the body image of women—and vice versa. We must come before the Lord to renew our thoughts and remember that we are created in His image.

ACTION: *Find one or two of the most provocative store windows that you can (try finding one that shows men or women as sexual objects in order to sell something. If this is an area of struggle for you, walk past the window and finish this station without looking at the window anymore). Stop to think through the values they are trying to communicate. Reflect on the difference between the image of people in the window, and the image of God in which we were created. Pray for your thought life to be renewed, and pray to be restored to God's image of who He made you to be.*

Scripture Reading Options

MATTHEW 5:27-30

You have heard that it was said, "Do not commit adultery." But I tell you that anyone who looks at a woman lustfully has already committed adultery with her in his heart. If your right eye causes you to sin, gouge it out and throw it away. It is better for you to lose one part of your body than for your whole body to be thrown into hell. And if your right hand causes you to sin, cut it off and throw it away. It is better for you to lose one part of your body than for your whole body to go into hell.

MATTHEW 6:22-23

The eye is the lamp of the body. If your eyes are good, your whole body will be full of light. But if your eyes are bad, your whole body will be full of darkness. If then the light within you is darkness, how great is that darkness!

GO DEEPER—ROMANS 12:2; EPHESIANS 4:17—5:2

Prayer Options

PRAYER OPTION 1:

Purify my heart, my God. Where we live, we are constantly under pressure to think that we should look like models and have bodies like people in pictures and in movies and the media. Lord, clear my mind of all that and remind me today that I am fearfully and wonderfully made by You—You love me as I am. Thank You, Lord.

PRAYER OPTION 2:

(Repeat this prayer: "Create in me a clean heart, O God. Renew a steadfast spirit within me.")

Key/Memory Verse

COLOSSIANS 3:9-10

You have taken off your old self with its practices and have put on the new self, which is being renewed in knowledge in the image of its Creator.

 ## STATION 5—FOOD COURT

This station is about fasting. Fasting is when we give up food for a meal or a day or longer in order to pray. Religious practices like fasting can be done with pure or false motives. We can try to "look religious" and impress people, or we can make a quiet sacrifice before God. Jesus gives specific instructions on fasting, mostly, that we do it for God not for the praise of people. It is our motives that matter.

ACTION: *Walk to the mall food court or restaurant and sit down. Instead of eating something, pray. Spend a few moments praying for those who are hungry, and praying again for the lost souls around you.*

This is your fast for the day. Talk to God about your spiritual disciplines and your motives.

Scripture Reading Options

MATTHEW 6:16-18

When you fast, do not look somber as the hypocrites do, for they disfigure their faces to show men they are fasting. I tell you the truth, they have received their reward in full. But when you fast, put oil on your head and wash your face, so that it will not be obvious to men that you are fasting, but only to your Father, who is unseen; and your Father, who sees what is done in secret, will reward you.

GO DEEPER—MATTHEW 6:25-26; ISAIAH 58:1-9

Prayer Options

PRAYER OPTION 1:

Lord Jesus, Your life was marked by sacrifice and surrender. You gave up everything for the sake of others. Lord, I struggle giving up just one meal so that I can pray and fast as You have asked us to do. Lord, make me more like You. I fast in my heart today, in the midst of abundance all around me, I choose to go without so that I can be more like You.

PRAYER OPTION 2:

Lord Jesus, I admit that sometimes I do religious things so that I may look like a good Christian. But this is not the kind of practice You have called me to do. You want a pure heart and pure motives— You aren't looking for outward religious followers—You are looking for true followers, who will worship You in spirit and in truth. I lay my false motives down. I surrender. I want to be real. Make me a true follower of You, Jesus.

Key/Memory Verse

MATTHEW 7:13-14

Don't look for shortcuts to God. The market is flooded with surefire, easygoing formulas for a successful life that can be practiced in your spare time. Don't fall for that stuff, even though crowds of people do. The way to life—to God!—is vigorous and requires total attention. (TM)

STATION 6—A TRENDY CLOTHING STORE

How much do you worry about what you have to wear? Our clothes are one of the main ways the world has determined whether or not we "fit in." Like jewelry, an abundance of food, and the car we drive—fashion and clothing are another way we can become trapped by the materialism of our culture. We often seek to acquire a closet full of clothes, and yet we feel we have nothing to wear. The truth is that we have plenty to wear, and much more than most of the rest of the world. The truth is that we have let the world shape us into its mold.

ACTION: *Stroll through this clothing store. Pick a few things out and go try them on. Note the total cost of the items you would like to purchase. If you feel comfortable, sit in the dressing room for the rest of this meditation in your "new" clothes. If not, put your old clothes on and find a place to sit outside of the store. Try to be alone, and let God lead you to a new understanding of spending money on yourself. Go back into that trendy store. Find a sales rack. Go ahead and tally up how much you could save if you bought only from the sales rack. Consider making a new covenant to purchase only items on sale and donating the savings to those in need.*

Scripture Reading Options

MATTHEW 6:28-30

And why do you worry about clothes? See how the lilies of the field grow. They do not labor or spin. Yet I tell you that not even Solomon in all his splendor was dressed like one of these. If that is how God clothes the grass of the field, which is here today and tomorrow is thrown into the fire, will he not much more clothe you, O you of little faith?

GO DEEPER—ROMANS 6:8-14; EPHESIANS 2:1-9

Prayer Options

PRAYER OPTION 1:

Lord, I want the latest fashion in clothes. But even more, I want the clothes You provide. I want the inner beauty and strength that

You create within me. Provide me with the outward and inward wardrobe that draws people to my character, my joy, and even my peace.

PRAYER OPTION 2:

Lord, help me to understand that in the battle to overcome some of the materialism in my own life, it is not enough just to save money. I must also GIVE my savings to benefit Your Kingdom, or to care for those in need. Challenge my heart in this area, Lord. The world has shaped my mind and my values so it is difficult to separate myself from it. Help me, Lord.

Key/Memory Verse

ROMANS 13:14

Rather, clothe yourselves with the Lord Jesus Christ, and do not think about how to gratify the desires of the sinful nature.

 ## STATION 7—PASSING PEOPLE BY

When our minds are full of distractions and we are busy following after our own wants and desires, it is easy to miss what is going on with the people around us. We can see this easily at the mall, where our senses are overloaded, there are so many things to see, so many people walking by, so many things to get—we can forget what it means to be a servant of all.

ACTION: *Spend five minutes walking through a crowded corridor of the mall. Notice as many people as you can as you walk. Do very many make eye contact? Try saying hello to one or two as you walk past. Then find a bench in that busy hallway, and prayerfully think about what it means to care for others, and to serve them—even if they are strangers. Spend some time talking with God about how you relate to those around you and how you treat other people.*

Scripture Reading Options

MATTHEW 5:38-39

You have heard that it was said, "Eye for eye, and tooth for tooth." But I tell you, Do not resist an evil person. If someone strikes you on the right cheek, turn to him the other also.

MATTHEW 7:1-2

Do not judge, or you too will be judged. For in the same way you judge others, you will be judged, and with the measure you use, it will be measured to you.

GO DEEPER—MATTHEW 5:43-48

Prayer Options

PRAYER OPTION 1:

Lord, when I think of the times that I have been hurt by people, I find myself asking, "Do I have to forgive?" I don't know how or where to begin. It is hard for me to think of offering my other cheek to be hit when my right cheek is still stinging. Lord, I confess, I don't know how to forgive those that hurt me on purpose. Yet I know that You endured more suffering than I ever will—and You still forgave. Help me to forgive like that.

PRAYER OPTION 2:

Lord, it's easy to help my friends. But I want to help those I don't know, who might even reject me. I don't know if I can do it, but I know that You can help me. Please give me Your heart of grace and mercy that I may serve others the way You serve me.

Key/Memory Verse

MATTHEW 7:12

So in everything, do to others what you would have them do to you.

 ## STATION 8—THE TOY STORE

Toys not only provide fun, but they can teach us a valuable lesson about how we order our lives.

ACTION: *Go ahead and spend a few minutes playing in the toy store. Before you leave, see if you can find building blocks or something that you can stack. Look at all the different toys on the shelves to build with. Which look like the most fun? Which would build the best skyscraper? Stack some building blocks if you can. As you stack each block, label it for one area of your life (family, friends, school, hobbies, etc.). You are building your life out of all of its pieces. Then talk to God about what kind of foundation you are building your life upon.*

Scripture Reading Options

MATTHEW 7:24-25

Therefore everyone who hears these words of mine and puts them into practice is like a wise man who built his house on the rock. The rain came down, the streams rose, and the winds blew and beat against that house; yet it did not fall, because it had its foundation on the rock.

GO DEEPER—I CORINTHIANS 3:10-13

Prayer Options

PRAYER OPTION 1:

(Spend some time in silence listening to God. Ask Him to speak to you about the foundation of your life.)

PRAYER OPTION 2:

Lord Jesus, it is so easy to build our lives out of the wrong things, to put the pieces of our lives in the wrong order, to build on a weak foundation. But Lord, if I will hear Your Word, and put it into practice in my life, You have promised that my life will not come tumbling down when the storm hits. Lord, I set my life on the foundation of Your Word. Amen.

Key/Memory Verse

MATTHEW 7:24

Therefore everyone who hears these words of mine and puts them into practice is like a wise man who built his house on the rock.

 STATION 9—MALL EXIT

ACTION: *Walk back out to one of the mall exits (preferably the same one you came in). Sit for a moment reflecting on all you just experienced. Hopefully, the eyes of your heart are adjusting to a new, Kingdom-centered view of the world. Just sit and pray.*

Scripture Reading Options

MATTHEW 6:9-13

This, then, is how you should pray: "Our Father in heaven, hallowed be your name, your kingdom come, your will be done on earth as it is in heaven. Give us today our daily bread. Forgive us our debts, as we also have forgiven our debtors. And lead us not into temptation, but deliver us from the evil one."

Prayer Options

PRAYER OPTION 1:

(Pray the Lord's Prayer, from Matthew 6:9-13.)

PRAYER OPTION 2:

My Savior and God, I trade the values of the world for Your values. I come to You and pray that You would renew my heart and mind that I may live Your Word and be a light in this world. Stamp Your image on my heart, and help me to walk in Your ways. Amen.

Key/Memory Verse

MATTHEW 7:13-14

Enter through the narrow gate. For wide is the gate and broad is the road that leads to destruction, and many enter through it. But small is the gate and narrow the road that leads to life, and only a few find it.

MEDITATION FOR THE CAMPUS

BY CHAP CLARK

The campus can be a tough place for most—the pressure to perform, the need to keep relationships going, wondering how others look at us. When we arrive on campus, no matter if it is middle school, high school, or college, we can be so preoccupied with making our way through the day that the last thing on our mind is our relationship with the Lord. Add to that the fact that the people of God can easily feel a bit odd and a little different from everybody else, and we are faced with tough struggles. All of this adds up to an internal struggle with what it means to follow Christ while in school.

The benefit of spending time devotionally with the campus in mind is that it can be a great reminder that Jesus is there, on campus, and has always been there. He cares about every person in the school and is watching over the school. He guards the gate and carefully watches each student, teacher, janitor, coach, and administrator. Our God is not afraid of or alarmed by what goes on at school—He knows it all, and He is on the move to bring His message of hope and healing to every person who walks the halls. And no school can keep Him off campus because He is everywhere.

The aim of this meditation is to remind student journeyers of these things: God is real, He is present, and He cares about each person in their school. He is there, and He is active. Meditating on this will help students live more confidently as His salt and light in the midst of those Christ loves and died for. Lunchtime, break time, after class—anytime is a good time to connect with God on campus.

 ## STATION I—GATE/MAIN ENTRANCE

To begin this meditation, we start at an entrance to the campus. Every day, it is the entrance for students, and for this meditation, it is the place where we will begin our move into Christ's presence.

The daily campus entrance can bring fear to some—they are entering a place where they may face rejection, failure, or worse. The campus can sometimes feel like an unsafe place. But the Lord is there. The gate does not keep Him out. There is no need to fear. The Lord is with us.

ACTION: *Walk to a campus entrance or gate. Talk to God about everything you face as you enter campus. Read through the "Scripture Reading Options," then walk through the entrance/gate.*

Scripture Reading Options

DEUTERONOMY 31:6

Be strong and courageous. Do not be afraid or terrified because of them, for the LORD your God goes with you; he will never leave you nor forsake you.

GO DEEPER—ISAIAH 2:4

Prayer Options

PRAYER OPTION 1:

Lord Jesus, help me to come to You honestly. Help me to turn my rambling thoughts to You. Let me rest my burdens on Your shoulders. I just want to be with You, for a short time this day, in a place where I spend my days. Walk with me, I pray.

PRAYER OPTION 2:

My Savior and my God, take away my fear, remind me that You are with me. Grant me courage to sustain me. I enter with You by my side. You are always with me. Thank You, Lord.

Key/Memory Verse

MATTHEW 11:28-30

Come to me, all you who are weary and burdened, and I will give you rest. Take my yoke upon you and learn from me, for I am gentle and humble in heart, and you will find rest for your souls. For my yoke is easy and my burden is light.

STATION 2—FIELD/GYM

When we compete in athletics for a school, we strive in the name of the school. We are usually part of a team, working together to bring honor not for ourselves, but for the school. When we serve in the kingdom of God, it is much the same. We work together with others to honor God and not ourselves.

ACTION: *Go to an athletic field or inside the gym. Think of some of those who practice and compete and the time they put in to be able to be their best and work together with their teammates. Consider who are your spiritual teammates. Think about your role in the Kingdom. Have you been trying to bring glory to yourself? Who can you serve for the Kingdom? Talk to God about being an obedient servant to all.*

Scripture Reading Options

PHILIPPIANS 3:14

I press on toward the goal to win the prize for which God has called me heavenward in Christ Jesus.

GO DEEPER—PHILIPPIANS 2:1-8; I CORINTHIANS 12:12, 14-15, 18

Prayer Options

PRAYER OPTION 1:

Dear God, help me to understand that I am not in competition with others. You love us all—we do not need to compete for a place in Your Kingdom. Allow me to participate in Your Kingdom work. Let me a part of Your team. Teach me what that means. Help me to serve those around me and not try to put myself first. Make my heart like that of Jesus. Make me a servant.

PRAYER OPTION 2:

Father, grant me discipline, time, and focus in my walk with You. May I become a disciplined disciple of Jesus, putting in the training time so that I will always be prepared to be Your servant. I humble myself. Teach me, Lord. Coach me. Show me what I need to work on in my life that I may grow and develop for Your service.

Key/Memory Verse

MARK 9:35

Sitting down, Jesus called the Twelve and said, "If anyone wants to be first, he must be the very last, and the servant of all."

 ## STATION 3—GROUPS

There are groups all over campus—social groups that have joined together to share a common interest or to have a set of friends to belong to so they don't have to be alone. Being on campus means belonging to a group of friends, and dealing with all the other campus groups. For this station, honestly consider how you feel about the various groups on campus—how you treat them and are treated by them.

ACTION: *Identify as many different groups that you can think of. Walk to a hangout location of one of the campus groups. Sit and observe from a distance. Consider what group or groups you are a part of. Pray for your groups of friends. Then talk to God about the groups that you are the most distant from—and maybe don't even like. Then think for a moment of those groups that you simply ignore, those you normally don't pay any attention to. Remember that God sees them and cares for them. Ask God to help you see others the way He sees them.*

Scripture Reading Options

2 TIMOTHY 1:4

Recalling your tears, I long to see you, so that I may be filled with joy.

LUKE 6:27

But I tell you who hear me: Love your enemies, do good to those who hate you.

2 CORINTHIANS 5:16

So from now on we regard no one from a worldly point of view. Though we once regarded Christ in this way, we do so no longer.

Prayer Options

PRAYER OPTION 1:

Heavenly Father, thanks for my friends. I pray that I may know that their love is but a reflection of Your love. Thank You for a group of people who love and accept me. Thank You for a group where I belong. I pray that You would help me to love them as You love them. Amen.

PRAYER OPTION 2:

Lord God, grant me compassion, understanding, and a welcoming heart. Fill me with Your love, so much so that my life would overflow with Your love. I pray that I would begin to understand and accept those who are different from me and those who I only see from a distance. You pour Your love and mercy on all—may I be like You.

Key/Memory Verse

LUKE 6:27

But I tell you who hear me: Love your enemies, do good to those who hate you.

 ## STATION 4—CAFETERIA/QUAD/STUDENT CENTER

On every campus, there is always a place for students to gather and relax—and to eat. We need nourishment and we need company. But there are always choices. We can choose what to put into our body, and we can choose with whom to spend our time. Both have a great impact on our development.

ACTION: *Go to the cafeteria or student center. Take a few moments to reflect on the choices we make about what we put into our bodies. Then consider the choices we make about who we allow to be our companions on our journey. What do we take into our lives? Who do we let in? Finally, picture communion, the bread and the cup. Remember for a moment the words of Jesus—"Take this and eat, for this is my body . . . Take and drink for this is my blood" (Matt. 26:26-28). Reflect on what it means for Jesus to be our bread and drink—and our friend. Talk to God about what it means for you to go out into the world and be a friend and support for others.*

Scripture Reading Options

JOHN 6:35

Then Jesus declared, "I am the bread of life. He who comes to me will never go hungry, and he who believes in me will never be thirsty."

I CORINTHIANS 15:33

Do not be misled: "Bad company corrupts good character."

JOHN 20:21

Again Jesus said, "Peace be with you! As the Father has sent me, I am sending you."

GO DEEPER—JOHN 6:25-59

Prayer Options

PRAYER OPTION 1:

Father, I believe that Jesus is the bread that makes us live. He is real food, He is our nourishment. Without Jesus we would starve spiritually. It is by His broken body and shed blood that we live. I thank You for offering Jesus to us to be our spiritual daily bread.

PRAYER OPTION 2:

(Repeat this prayer, "Father God, help me to be 'bread' to the world, as Christ is bread to me.")

Key/Memory Verse

JOHN 6:35

Then Jesus declared, "I am the bread of life. He who comes to me will never go hungry, and he who believes in me will never be thirsty."

 STATION 5—EMPTY CLASS/DESKS

Life is more about *learning* than *doing*. While we are in school, we learn both inside and outside the classroom. In both places, there are tests as well. Not everything that happens in life is a test, but there are times that we do face tests. A test is simply the way we see our progress. In school we test our mind; in life we tests our hearts. If we are willing to sit and learn, God has much to teach us.

sacred space

ACTION: *Find an empty classroom and sit at a desk. Try to think of as many things as you can that you learned in class this week. Then try to think of what you have learned about life this week. Ask God to teach you and build your character. Talk to Him about applying His Word to your life.*

Scripture Reading Options

JOHN 5:39-40

You diligently study the Scriptures because you think that by them you possess eternal life. These are the Scriptures that testify about me, yet you refuse to come to me to have life.

PSALM 26:2-3

Test me, O LORD, and try me, examine my heart and my mind; for your love is ever before me, and I walk continually in your truth.

GO DEEPER—2 TIMOTHY 3:14-15

Prayer Options

PRAYER OPTION 1:

Lord God, give me a fresh desire to be open to learning new things. Teach me by Your Spirit. Build my character and integrity, so that when I am tested my life will bring glory to You, Lord.

PRAYER OPTION 2:

I want to know You, Jesus. More than anything else, more than any other knowledge, I want to know You. Help me to be a better disciple—a better learner of You and Your ways. Help me to be obedient to what You have already shown me.

Key/Memory Verse

PSALM 139:23-25

Search me, O God, and know my heart; test me and know my anxious thoughts. See if there is any offensive way in me, and lead me in the way everlasting.

 ## STATION 6—LOCKERS (DORM ROOM)

At this station we will take a look deep within. Our lockers (or dorm room closet) become a place where we store things, hide things, lock things away. It becomes a symbol of something that we do as human beings—we try to hide things away hoping that God won't see them. What do you have packed away inside?

ACTION: *Walk to a place where you can see some of the campus lockers (or go to your dorm room or a dorm lobby). Think about the kinds of things we put into lockers and closets. What "treasures" do we try to lock away so that we can hold on to them? Sit for a few moments and open your heart before God. Allow Him to point out to you anything that you have been hiding from Him, or have tried to lock up, out of His reach. What is in the dark corner of your closet or locker? Open the door, let the light in and confess it to God and receive His forgiveness and mercy.*

Scripture Reading Options

MARK 4:22

For whatever is hidden is meant to be disclosed, and whatever is concealed is meant to be brought out into the open.

LUKE 12:33-34

Sell your possessions and give to the poor. Provide purses for yourselves that will not wear out, a treasure in heaven that will not be exhausted, where no thief comes near and no moth destroys. For where your treasure is, there your heart will be also.

GO DEEPER—LUKE 18:18-30

Prayer Options

PRAYER OPTION 1:

(Spend some time with God, allowing Him to speak to you about trading earthly treasures for heavenly ones. Ask Him to show you one specific way that you could do that this week.)

PRAYER OPTION 2:

God, You will eventually bring all things into the light, why do I try to hide from You? Shine Your light on the dark spaces in my soul. Help me to "clean house" so that I have nothing hidden from You.

Key/Memory Verse

LUKE 12:34

For where your treasure is, there your heart will be also.

 ## STATION 7—SIGN OUT FRONT/FLAGPOLE

The sign in front of a campus usually will have the school name, school colors, and often the mascot. There is no mistaking where you are. This raises the question—what does my sign say about me? If I am one of God's letters to the world, what do they know about God from me? What colors are on my flag? Does my sign tell others about the living Christ? My sign (or flag) is the thing that identifies the One to whom I belong.

ACTION: *Walk to the campus front sign or flagpole. Talk to God about what your sign or flag tells others about who you are and to whom you belong. Ask God what He would like your sign or flag to say.*

Scripture Reading Options

MATTHEW 5:14

You are the light of the world. A city on a hill cannot be hidden.

I PETER 3:15

But in your hearts set apart Christ as Lord. Always be prepared to give an answer to everyone who asks you to give the reason for the hope that you have. But do this with gentleness and respect.

GO DEEPER—2 CORINTHIANS 3:2-3

Prayer Options

PRAYER OPTION 1:

(Repeat this verse as a prayer, "You are the light of the world.")

PRAYER OPTION 2:

Lord, make me someone whose words are filled with "gentleness and respect." Help me to live in such a way that people will ask me about You. And when they ask, let my words be full of gentleness and respect, and may all I say and do reflect Your character.

Key/Memory Verse

MATTHEW 5:14

You are the light of the world. A city on a hill cannot be hidden.

MEDITATION FOR THE OUTDOORS

BY ED ROBINSON

A poet once wrote that "every common bush is afire with God." God has filled the outdoors with "God signs." Creation is crammed with evidence of God's hand. When we look for the "holy" in the outdoors, we see a God who puts His signature on everything. We can sense God's presence and hear God's voice in the blowing wind, the cool rain, or the warm sunshine.

We're also part of God's creation. We aren't just souls or spirits who live in bodies. When we exert energy (e.g., walking, rock climbing, or rollerblading), we understand more about ourselves as "fearfully and wonderfully made." We feel our muscles, our breathing, and the rhythms of our heartbeat. When we stop to listen, feel, and reflect outdoors, we begin to understand that God is present and speaking there.

On this journey of prayer and reflection in the outdoors, you will see things you've already seen, hear familiar sounds, and feel things you've felt before. But, this time, be prepared to see, hear, and feel God in them. In the process, you may discover that you not only know God better, but yourself as well.

 ## STATION I—THE SKY: GOD'S DECLARATION OF GREATNESS

The sky seems endless. Though it's possible to calculate some of its expanse, it is impossible to see the whole sky from where you stand. Imagine the expanse as the declaration of God's glory.

ACTION: *Try looking just at the sky without seeing anything else on the horizon. Lie down on your back and look up. Watch the movement of the clouds and the wind. Sense the warmth of the sun. If it's early evening, watch as the stars emerge. Don't be in a hurry.*

Scripture Reading Options

ISAIAH 45:5-7

I am the LORD, and there is no other; apart from me there is no God . . . from the rising of the sun to the place of its setting men may know there is none besides me. I am the LORD, and there is no other. I form the light and create darkness, I bring prosperity and create disaster; I, the LORD, do all these things.

PSALM 19:1-2

The heavens declare the glory of God; the skies proclaim the work of his hands. Day after day they pour forth speech; night after night they display knowledge.

GO DEEPER—ACTS 1:9-11

Prayer Options

PRAYER OPTION 1:

Lord, Your power is evident in the expanse of the sky. To imagine that You sustain the rising and the setting of the sun, the perfect rotation of the earth, the patterns of seasons that match with the time for resting, planting, growing, and harvesting—to think that You made all this and still care personally for me may be the most powerful thing of all. Amen.

PRAYER OPTION 2:

Lord, the skies "speak" everyday, everywhere, to everyone. What do You want me to hear from You today? What do You want me to know of Your love, Your power, and Your care—not only for creation as a whole, but for me? Quiet my heart so I will be able to hear You speak rather than watching clouds and counting stars and miss the divine message they are designed to deliver. Amen.

Key/Memory Verse

PSALM 19:1

The heavens declare the glory of God; the skies proclaim the work of his hands.

STATION 2—THE HORIZON: GETTING THE BIG PICTURE

Even when working on details, God always paints on a big canvas so that eventually we get the "big picture" of His salvation story. When we make the effort to look at the horizon rather than the small space immediately around us, we can see what God sees.

ACTION: *Find a place you can stand or sit and see the horizon. You may have to move to get the best view. Let you eyes go from one end of the horizon to the other. Don't focus on the details. Get the big picture. Reflect on some of your experiences where God was working in your life but you didn't know it at the time. You only saw the immediate situation you were in. Image that the horizon represents God's "big picture" of grace at work in you.*

Scripture Reading Options

PSALM 121:1-2

I look up to the mountains—does my help come from there? My help comes from the LORD, who made the heavens and the earth! (NLT)

ISAIAH 40:12

Who has measured the waters in the hollow of his hand, or with the breadth of his hand marked off the heavens? Who has held the dust of the earth in a basket, or weighed the mountains on the scales and the hills in a balance?

GO DEEPER—PSALM 121:1-8; ROMANS 8:35-39

Prayer Options

PRAYER OPTION 1:

Lord, why is it that I often look down at my situations trying to find my own way? Why is it that You are the last place I look after I've tried everything else? You are my best help in every situation. Your eyes never leave me. Your guiding hand is never too busy that You can't touch my life. Help me to look to You no matter what I may be going through. Amen.

PRAYER OPTION 2:

Lord, how majestic Your creation is, and You and You alone created it all! I'm awed that You are the One who also created me and loves me! Your creative work doesn't end with land, water, plants, animals, or even humans. Your creativity continues daily in the ways You renew my life and lead me in the way You want me to go. Make me new and give me courage to follow You today. Amen.

Key/Memory Verse

PSALM 113:3

From the rising of the sun to the place where it sets, the name of the LORD is to be praised.

 ### STATION 3—A PATH: A METAPHOR FOR LIFE

Life is a journey on a path. Sometimes the paths are old and well traveled. Sometimes the paths are brand-new and the traveler is a trailblazer. Sometimes the path is straight and well marked. Sometimes the path is crooked or unclear and you have to pay attention to find where to go. That's life.

ACTION: *Observe the paths, walkways, and roads where you are. Stand in the middle of a path and look ahead and then look behind. The path comes from someplace and leads to somewhere. As you meditate on your life, think about the spiritual path you're on. How clear is the way? In your meditation, remember that there isn't any life path that God has not already gone before you.*

Scripture Reading Options

PROVERBS 4:18, 25-27

The path of the righteous is like the first gleam of dawn, shining ever brighter till the full light of day. . . . Let your eyes look straight ahead, fix your gaze directly before you. Make level paths for your feet and take only ways that are firm. Do not swerve to the right or the left; keep your foot from evil.

GO DEEPER—PSALM 23:1-6; LUKE 10:30-37

Prayer Options

PRAYER OPTION 1:

Lord, there are so many different paths to choose in life. The number of choices leaves me tired and confused. How can I say thanks for the way You lead me? For although You leave the choice of which path to take up to me, You are faithful to show me which ones are best. Just like a shepherd leads the sheep on the right path, You are a shepherd to me. I feel safe with You. Amen.

PRAYER OPTION 2:

Lord, You never intended for me to "find my own path." You don't want me to wander around in the darkness trying to figure out which way to go. You have a level path designed for me. Give me the faith to trust You with the direction of that path. Grant me courage to stay on that path, even when I can't see or fully understand where it goes. Amen.

Key/Memory Verse

PROVERBS 3:5-6

Trust in the LORD with all your heart and lean not on your own understanding; in all your ways acknowledge him, and he will make your paths straight.

 ## STATION 4—ROCK AND STONES

Rock solid . . . hard as rock . . . steady as a rock. Natural rock is firm and unyielding. Stones are also made out of rock. Amassed together, stones can be used for building, but they can also be thrown to break and hurt people and things. How do you use rocks in your life, for building or throwing?

ACTION: *Look around and find a rock formation. Consider its strength. As you observe the rock remember that one of the names by which Jesus is known is "the Solid Rock." Take a minute and allow your feet to feel the ground beneath them. Consider whether you are standing on solid rock or on a shaky foundation. Find a stone and hold it in your hand. Take a moment to reflect on the "stones" that you have thrown to hurt others—and the stones that have been thrown at you.*

Scripture Reading Options

PSALM 62:1-2

My soul finds rest in God alone; my salvation comes from him. He alone is my rock and my salvation; he is my fortress, I will never be shaken.

GO DEEPER—JOHN 8:3-11

Prayer Options

PRAYER OPTION 1:

Lord, so many people are trying to find something in their lives that will last. They try all sorts of things hoping they will find something that will be good enough and strong enough to give true meaning and purpose to their lives. I'm glad that You are the most enduring thing in my life. You are my rock and my salvation. As long as I have You I don't need to try anything else. You are enough! Amen.

PRAYER OPTION 2:

Lord, I've seen a lot of "stone-throwing" in my life. I've even thrown a few stones at people myself. Sometimes I make quick judgments about people instead of looking at them as You do. Forgive me, Lord. I don't want to be known as a "stone-thrower." I'd rather be more like Christ and be an agent of forgiveness, healing, and reconciliation. Next time I'm tempted to "cast the first stone," remind me of my commitment to be like You. Amen.

Key/Memory Verse

MATTHEW 7:24

Therefore everyone who hears these words of mine and puts them into practice is like a wise man who built his house on the rock.

 STATION 5—DIRT: A FRAGILE STRENGTH

Scripture has a lot to say about dirt. Dirt is used to explain the fact that human physical life doesn't last forever . . . "returning to dust" is what many people call it. Sometimes dirt (particularly when people owned land) was used as a way of illustrating God's blessing to people who followed and obeyed Him. Sometimes soil is used in Jesus parables to describe the level of openness people have to the gospel.

ACTION: *Move to another location and grab a hand full of dirt. Feel its weight and texture. Look at its color. Think about how easy or hard it is to grow something in this kind of soil. Imagine that your life is like that soil—earthy, fragile, yet strong enough to grow character.*

Scripture Reading Options

GENESIS 3:17-19

To Adam he said, "Because you listened to your wife and ate from the tree about which I commanded you, 'You must not eat of it,' Cursed is the ground because of you; through painful toil you will eat of it all the days of your life. It will produce thorns and thistles for you, and you will eat the plants of the field. By the sweat of your brow you will eat your food until you return to the ground, since from it you were taken; for dust you are and to dust you will return."

ISAIAH 40:6-8

A voice says, "Cry out." And I said, "What shall I cry?" "All men are like grass, and all their glory is like the flowers of the field. The grass withers and the flowers fall, because the breath of the LORD blows on them. Surely the people are grass. The grass withers and the flowers fall, but the word of our God stands forever."

GO DEEPER—MARK 4:2-9

Prayer Options

PRAYER OPTION 1:

Lord, sometimes I feel strong, almost indestructible. I guess that's what You must feel like all the time. But I'm not You. You are the Creator and I'm just a creature. You are absolutely unlimited and I'm limited by time, space, and power. Forgive me when I try to make myself out to be more than I really am. Help me to realize that I am but dust, and whatever strength I do have comes as a gift from You. Even though I sometimes act like it, God, I don't want Your job. Amen.

PRAYER OPTION 2:

Lord, sometimes life seems so fragile. So much is changing so quickly. It seems like my life is withering away even though I'm still young. Thank You for reminding me that my life doesn't depend on me. It depends on You. You don't wither away. Your truth doesn't change. Maybe my life isn't as fragile as I thought. My times are in Your hands. Amen.

Key/Memory Verse

LUKE 8:15

But the seed on good soil stands for those with a noble and good heart, who hear the word, retain it, and by persevering produce a crop.

STATION 6—FOOTPRINTS: BACK TO THE FUTURE

Unless you're standing in a place where no one's ever been before there is probably some sign that someone else has already been where you're standing. Consider the people who've left their "footprints" in your spiritual life. What kind of contribution did/do they make? As you follow in their steps, what kind of an impact would you like to have on someone who will come after you?

ACTION: *Walk to a nearby location where you can find a sign that another person was there. Look especially for a human footprint. If you find one, look at the print. Try to imagine what that person was/is like—are they male, female, large, small, old, young? Leave your own footprint for someone else who will come after you. Consider those who have left their "mark" on your life. Now consider the "mark" you are leaving behind.*

Scripture Reading Options

PSALM 37:23-24

If the LORD delights in a man's way, he makes his steps firm; though he stumble, he will not fall, for the LORD upholds him with his hand.

I TIMOTHY 4:12, 16

Don't let anyone look down on you because you are young, but set an example for the believers in speech, in life, in love, in faith and in purity . . . Watch your life and doctrine closely. Persevere in them, because if you do, you will save both yourself and your hearers.

GO DEEPER—I JOHN I:5—2:6

Prayer Options

PRAYER OPTION I:

Lord, I have great models of faithful Christians in my life. They are living testimonies of Your faithfulness. Sometimes when I wonder about what to do, I think about what they've done and I try to do the same thing. You're really good to provide me with their spiritual footprints. Amen.

PRAYER OPTION 2:

Lord, even though I'm young, You want me to show others how to be Your disciple. I want that too. Help my footprints to be clear enough, straight enough, and strong enough that other people can follow me as I follow You. Help them not to see me, but to see You in me. Amen.

Key/Memory Verse

I JOHN 2:6

Whoever claims to live in him must walk as Jesus did.

 ## STATION 7—WATER: IN THE STREAM OF GOD'S GRACE

Water means life in the physical world. Where there's water, things grow and live. Where there's no water, things wither and die. They die of thirst. The same thing is true in the spiritual world. People can die of spiritual thirst as well. But they don't need to. Jesus said He was the living water, available to everyone.

ACTION: *Look for evidences of water around you (e.g., pond, stream, puddle). Notice any plant growth in the vicinity of the water; then notice its color. Consider how the water of God's grace keeps the spiritual growth in your life alive.*

Scripture Reading Options

ISAIAH 35:4, 6-8

Be strong, do not fear; your God will come . . . Water will gush forth in the wilderness and streams in the desert. The burning sand will become a pool, the thirsty ground bubbling springs. In the haunts where jackals once lay, grass and reeds and papyrus will grow. And a highway will be there; it will be called the Way of Holiness.

JOHN 7:37-39

On the last and greatest day of the Feast, Jesus stood and said in a loud voice, "If anyone is thirsty, let him come to me and drink. Whoever believes in me, as the Scripture has said, streams of living water will flow from within him." By this he meant the Spirit, whom those who believed in him were later to re-

ceive. Up to that time the Spirit had not been given, since Jesus had not yet been glorified.

GO DEEPER—MATTHEW 25:35-40

Prayer Options

PRAYER OPTION 1:

Lord, sometimes my life feels like a desert. But that's exactly the kind of place where You love to pour out the water of Your grace in order to show people how You can transform the dryness of their life. Help me to trust You to put streams in my desert. That's what I really need. Amen.

PRAYER OPTION 2:

The water of Your grace isn't just for me. It's for everyone else too. Open my eyes to see those around me who need a drink of Your living water today in their lives. Help me remember that I can bring them a cup of cold water in Your name, to quench their spiritual thirst. Let my life be a spring overflowing with Your living water. Amen.

Key/Memory Verse

PSALM 63:1

O God, you are my God, earnestly I seek you; my soul thirsts for you, my body longs for you, in a dry and weary land where there is no water.

 ### STATION 8—ROOTS: HOW DEEP DO YOURS GO DOWN?

Roots are one of the ways that trees and plants get the water and nutrients they need to live and grow. Roots also keep trees and plants from falling over in a storm. The deeper the roots, the stronger the plant. Our lives need roots, deep roots, if we are going to get what we need to grow spiritually and survive some of the challenges life throws our way.

ACTION: *You may have to look hard, but try and find a tree or plant that has some of its roots exposed. Imagine how wide and deep the rest of the root system must go. Think about the roots in your own life. How did they get there? How far do they go down? Prayerfully consider the depth of your own roots.*

Scripture Reading Options

PSALM 1:1-3

Blessed is the man who does not walk in the counsel of the wicked or stand in the way of sinners or sit in the seat of mockers. But his delight is in the law of the LORD, and on his law he meditates day and night. He is like a tree planted by streams of water, which yields its fruit in season and whose leaf does not wither. Whatever he does prospers.

MATTHEW 13:3-6

Then he told them many things in parables, saying: "A farmer went out to sow his seed. As he was scattering the seed, some fell along the path, and the birds came and ate it up. Some fell on rocky places, where it did not have much soil. It sprang up quickly, because the soil was shallow. But when the sun came up, the plants were scorched, and they withered because they had no root."

GO DEEPER—2 TIMOTHY 1:3-7

Prayer Options

PRAYER OPTION 1:

Lord, I want to live my life for You. I want my life to count for something that will last, not just make a big "show" and fade away. There are already too many people like that in the world. I want my roots to go down deep. Give me the patience and discipline to focus on what's underneath the surface as much as I focus on what can be seen. Amen.

PRAYER OPTION 2:

Lord, I don't want to build my life on anything that won't last. I know storms are inevitable. But I'm not interested in simply surviving the storms—I want to have peace in the middle of them. I know that can only happen if I build my life on Christ and Your Word. Even houses that appear great collapse unless they're securely grounded on a solid foundation. I'd rather have a great foundation than a great house any day. Amen.

Key/Memory Verse

PSALM 1:1, 3

Blessed is the man who does not walk in the counsel of the wicked . . . He is like a tree planted by streams of water, which yields its fruit in season and whose leaf does not wither. Whatever he does prospers.

STATION 9—ONE SQUARE FOOT: EVIDENCE OF A PERSONAL GOD

God is not only the God of great things; He's also the God of little things. His power is just as great when applied to the small things in life that we sometimes think are "too small" for God to be concerned about.

ACTION: *Find one square foot of ground that looks interesting. Sit or lay down where you can focus on the small details in the one square foot. What do you see . . . a blade of grass, a small bug, grains of sand? Just as you're focused on the tiny details in the one square foot, consider how concerned God is for the details of your one solitary life.*

Scripture Reading Options

MATTHEW 10:29-31

Are not two sparrows sold for a penny? Yet not one of them will fall to the ground apart from the will of your Father. And even the very hairs of your head are all numbered. So don't be afraid; you are worth more than many sparrows.

COLOSSIANS 1:15-17

He is the image of the invisible God, the firstborn over all creation. For by him all things were created: things in heaven and on earth, visible and invisible, whether thrones or powers or rulers or authorities; all things were created by him and for him. He is before all things, and in him all things hold together.

GO DEEPER—JOHN 4:7-10, 16-26

Prayer Options

PRAYER OPTION 1:

Lord, I spend a lot of time thinking about the small stuff . . . clothes, school, job, and others' opinions. I know these aren't bad things; they're just not the most important things. Help me to not get so caught up with them that I forget about You. Amen.

PRAYER OPTION 2:

Lord, You know me better than I know myself. You know the personal details of my life just like You knew the hidden details of the life of the Samaritan woman. Even if I try to hide things from my friends, family, and myself—You know. Help me to know that even though You know, or maybe because You know, You love me and want to forgive, heal, and make those details new. Amen.

Key/Memory Verse

PSALM 139:23

Search me, O God, and know my heart.

 STATION 10—THE SEED: DYING TO LIVE

Only dying seeds produce fruit. That's the way seeds work. The best seed in the world won't produce anything if it stays attached to the plant and refuses to let go. It will never reach the ground to germinate and produce other plants.

ACTION: *Look for seeds. You may see them dangling from a tree, in the blossom of a flower, or blowing in the wind. They're waiting to die so they can live again as a new tree, plant, or flower. Our spiritual lives are surprisingly like that, aren't they? Take a few minutes, hold a seed in your hand, and reflect on how the life of Christ was like a seed and how your life is like a seed.*

Scripture Reading Options

MARK 4:30-32

Again he said, "What shall we say the kingdom of God is like, or what parable shall we use to describe it? It is like a mustard seed, which is the smallest seed you plant in the ground. Yet when planted, it grows and becomes the largest of all garden plants, with such big branches that the birds of the air can perch in its shade."

JOHN 12:23-25

Jesus replied, "The hour has come for the Son of Man to be glorified. I tell you the truth, unless a kernel of wheat falls to the ground and dies, it remains only a single seed. But if it dies, it produces many seeds. The man who loves his life will lose it, while the man who hates his life in this world will keep it for eternal life."

GO DEEPER—GALATIANS 2:19-21

Prayer Options

PRAYER OPTION 1:

Lord, it is amazing how You are able to make things grow not only in the physical world, but in the spiritual world as well. I don't know why I should be surprised by that, but sometimes when I think about what You've done in my life and the life of my friends, it's more than I can contain. I just want to say "Alleluia." I believe and know that You are not finished with me yet. Amen.

PRAYER OPTION 2:

Lord, I can't fully comprehend the depth of love You have for me that You should send Jesus to die for me. But even though I don't fully understand it, I believe it! Jesus was the kernel of wheat that died alone, but His death saved millions of people, including me. Thank You. Amen.

Key/Memory Verse

JOHN 12:24

Unless a kernel of wheat falls to the ground and dies, it remains only a single seed. But if it dies, it produces many seeds.

 ## STATION 11—A TREE OR PLANT: MAKING YOUR LIFE COUNT

Plants produce other plants. Trees produce other trees. Vegetation creates more vegetation. That's nature's plan. Consider that plants represent God's provision for our spiritual lives—we are spiritual plants that are created to bear spiritual fruit.

ACTION: *Observe the trees and plants in your immediate area. Look at their differences. See if you can find evidence of the various species reproducing themselves. Can you spot the next generation of plants already growing without any human assistance? Spend a moment to consider that God is at work in your life—even when you can't see it.*

Scripture Reading Options

MATTHEW 7:17-20

Likewise every good tree bears good fruit, but a bad tree bears bad fruit. A good tree cannot bear bad fruit, and a bad tree cannot bear good fruit. Every tree that does not bear good fruit is cut down and thrown into the fire. Thus, by their fruit you will recognize them.

John 15:4-5

Remain in me, and I will remain in you. No branch can bear fruit by itself; it must remain in the vine. Neither can you bear fruit unless you remain in me. I am the vine; you are the branches. If a man remains in me and I in him, he will bear much fruit; apart from me you can do nothing

Go Deeper—Psalm 104:1-18; Genesis 1:9-13

Prayer Options

Prayer Option 1:

When I look at all the trees and plants around me here, I remember that You placed the first humans in a garden where You gave them everything they needed to live. You asked them to take care of that garden. That's still the way it works, isn't it, God? You provide for our every need, and You ask us to join You in caring for Your creation. May I be as "re-creative" as You are. Amen.

Prayer Option 2:

Lord, I guess I should not expect to produce any kind of fruit other than what is present in my own life. Sometimes I wonder what kind of fruit is actually coming out of my life. I want it to be good, but I'm not always sure it is. Would You make me more like You so that the fruit of my life will look like the fruit of the Spirit? That's really what I want. Amen.

Key/Memory Verse

John 15:5

I am the vine; you are the branches. If a man remains in me and I in him, he will bear much fruit; apart from me you can do nothing.

 ## STATION 12—BREATH: THE ESSENTIAL FOR LIFE

We don't usually "try" to breathe. We aren't aware of our own breath. We just breathe; its one of those involuntary reflexes. But today, think about your own breathing. Try different rhythms . . . inhale and exhale slowly. Feel the good air fill your lungs and the "used" air escape. If it's cold enough you may even be able to see your breath.

ACTION: *Walk slowly through an open area. Listen to your own breathing. Meditate on what the act of breathing means. Think about what it means when God "breathes" His life into us.*

Scripture Reading Options

GENESIS 2:7

The LORD God formed the man from the dust of the ground and breathed into his nostrils the breath of life, and the man became a living being.

JOHN 20:21-22

Again Jesus said, "Peace be with you! As the Father has sent me, I am sending you." And with that he breathed on them and said, "Receive the Holy Spirit."

GO DEEPER—ISAIAH 40:28-31; EZEKIEL 37:9-14

Prayer Options

PRAYER OPTION 1:

Lord, at times I feel so tired . . . tired of trying, tired of caring, tired of hoping, tired of loving, tired of believing. I'm tired of working so hard and seeing so little happen as a result of my efforts. I'm waiting now on You. Give me new strength. Breathe new energy so I will keep trying and maybe, if You want, go higher and farther than I've ever been before. Amen.

PRAYER OPTION 2:

Lord, there are so many dead things around me . . . relationships, families, friends, futures, even churches. They're still alive on the outside, but inside they're dead. Is it possible that You could breathe new life into them just like You did to the valley of bones? I believe You can. May it be according to Your will. Amen.

Key/Memory Verse

GENESIS 2:7

The LORD God formed the man from the dust of the ground and breathed into his nostrils the breath of life, and man became a living being.

MEDITATION FOR A MISSION TRIP

BY JIM HAMPTON

Whether you have chosen to go on a mission trip to another land, or you are just serving in your neighborhood, you've just engaged in one of the most transforming experiences in which a person can participate. Anytime you get involved in service or missions, you will have the opportunity to be radically changed by your experience.

Finding time to reflect on what God is doing in a setting of service can be difficult at best. Busy work schedules, being in a crowded van or bus, the absence of all the comforts of home, and even the needy people you encounter can actually keep you from taking the time necessary to stop and really consider what God is doing in your life and in the lives of those around you. You will have to look for an appropriate "down time," when things slow down, and make the time to get away to be with God.

 ## STATION I—HEART TRAINING (BIBLE)

Prior to any journey, there is preparation. Whether you realized it or not, you already had one of the primary training tools you needed—your Bible. Think back to the many lessons you've heard on missions and service. What does the Bible have to say about meeting the needs of others? What role do we play in that process? What role does God play? As you ponder these questions, remember that everything we need to prepare our hearts for His service can be found in the Bible. Consider the state of preparation of your heart. Have you spent time in the Word and let it speak to you and shape you? Take some time to reaffirm the Word of God as your foundation.

MEDITATION FOR A MISSION TRIP

ACTION: *Find a quiet location, pull out your Bible and look at it for a moment.*

Scripture Reading Options

2 Timothy 3:16-17

All Scripture is God-breathed and is useful for teaching, rebuking, correcting and training in righteousness, so that the man of God may be thoroughly equipped for every good work.

Matthew 4:1-4

Then Jesus was led by the Spirit into the desert to be tempted by the devil. After fasting forty days and forty nights, he was hungry. The tempter came to him and said, "If you are the Son of God, tell these stones to become bread." Jesus answered, "It is written: 'Man does not live on bread alone, but on every word that comes from the mouth of God.'"

Go Deeper—Psalm 119:97-105

Prayer Options

Prayer Option 1:

God of all knowledge, thank You for giving us Your written Word. It reminds us not only of what we are to be doing, but most importantly, it reaffirms for us that You are what is important, not us. It is Your story, O God, that is told in these pages. Would You regularly remind us that this story we are a part of is not about us, but all about You? Even when we are on a mission trip or involved in service, help us really understand that it isn't about anything that we have to contribute, but it is what You have already done for us and desire to do through us. May our every action reflect who You are. Amen.

Prayer Option 2:

O Lord, our Rock and Redeemer, we confess today that we are not lovers of Your law. For if we were, we would spend much more time studying Your commands, memorizing Your teachings, and living our lives according to Your desires. We ask Your forgiveness for our lack of commitment to Your Word. We pledge that we will invest ourselves anew in this living book so that we may come to know You better, and in so doing, know ourselves. Then we will be equipped to do the work You've called us to do as Your disciples. Amen.

Key/Memory Verse

MATTHEW 4:4

It is written: "Man does not live on bread alone, but on every word that comes from the mouth of God."

 ### STATION 2—TALENTS (TOOLS)

Missions and service utilize tools. Sometimes the tools are obvious—hammers, saws, screwdrivers. The tools may be Vacation Bible School (VBS) supplies, lesson books, sports equipment. Sometimes the tools may be nothing more than the ability to listen, to encourage, or to organize. It would be extremely hard to do a construction project if you didn't have a hammer to pound the nails in. (Your hand would be pretty sore after just a few blows!) Similarly, trying to run a VBS without the benefit of a lesson plan would be quite difficult. Consider for a moment the function and purpose of tools—both physical and spiritual.

ACTION: *Walk to a place where you can find some of the tools used to serve. Take a look around and, if possible, pick them up and consider how they are used. Reflect on the tools God has given you for service.*

Scripture Reading Options

MATTHEW 25:21

His master replied, "Well done, good and faithful servant! You have been faithful with a few things; I will put you in charge of many things. Come and share your master's happiness!"

JOB 1:21

The LORD gave, and the LORD hath taken away; blessed be the name of the LORD. (KJV)

GO DEEPER—EPHESIANS 2:10; 2 TIMOTHY 3:16-17

Prayer Options

PRAYER OPTION 1:

God of all good things, thank You for the tools You have given me and others to serve You. We are grateful that You trust us to use them to help others, and for the opportunity to participate in Your act of caring for the world. Thank You for Your trust in us. We know we don't always use our tools the way we should. Our prayer is that we would always use our tools for Your glory and to further the work of Your Kingdom here on earth. And as we do so, may You find great joy in us doing those things You created us to do. Amen.

Prayer Option 2:

God, we know that You give us tools for a purpose. We aren't to hoard them or hide them. Rather we are to use them for the sake of others. May we not be like the servant who hid his talents, and in the end, lost all he had. Instead, may we take the tools You have generously given to us according to our ability and use them in the service of others. In so doing, would You multiply our tools so that we can reach more people for You? We thank You in advance for Your help. Amen.

Key/Memory Verse

Matthew 5:14-16

You are the light of the world. A city on a hill cannot be hidden. Neither do people light a lamp and put it under a bowl. Instead they put it on its stand, and it gives light to everyone in the house. In the same way, let your light shine before men, that they may see your good deeds and praise your Father in heaven.

 ## STATION 3—COMMUNITY (TEAMWORK)

When you do missions or service, it quickly becomes apparent that it will take more than your efforts alone to make it work. You work together with a team to achieve certain things, things that no one person could do alone. Think about your involvement in missions and service and consider how different people's efforts were necessary to complete the task at hand. Every time you do something alongside someone else, remember to tell them "Thank you" for their contributions.

ACTION: *Walk far enough from your work area that you can look back on it. Try to find a place where you can see teammates, or coworkers, or others serving in ministry. Give prayerful thought to the need for* *a variety of talents and multiple sets of hands to do the work of ministry. Give thanks that God gives us brothers and sisters to serve alongside us—and He gives His Spirit to be present with us.*

Scripture Reading Options

ECCLESIASTES 4:12

Though one may be overpowered, two can defend themselves. A cord of three strands is not quickly broken.

JOHN 13:34-35

A new command I give you: Love one another. As I have loved you, so you must love one another. By this all men will know that you are my disciples, if you love one another.

GO DEEPER—I CORINTHIANS 12:12, 18, 26

Prayer Options

PRAYER OPTION 1:

God in three persons, Father, Son, and Holy Spirit—just as You are three-in-one, so You have made us with a built-in need for community and working together. Thank You for instilling in us the need to rely on others. May You daily remind us of just how important each person is to Your mission. Remind us of the incredible contributions each team member makes and how important it is that we work in harmony with one another. As we engage in Your work, may we become the cord that is not easily broken. Amen.

PRAYER OPTION 2:

Gracious God, Your Word tells us that You have made us like a body, such that each part has importance. As we seek to serve You, we stand in awe of the wonderful gifts each person has to offer and despair at our own contributions. Would You remind us that what we offer, no matter how small, has great importance to a team? Please help us to see that when our individual gifts are combined with the strengths of others it produces something far greater than we could ever imagine. Thank You for the gift of interdependence. May we always remember the necessity of caring for each other, especially those who have great need, so that the body may be whole. Amen.

Key/Memory Verse

GALATIANS 6:10

Therefore, as we have opportunity, let us do good to all people, especially to those who belong to the family of believers.

 ## STATION 4—IMAGE OF GOD (PEOPLE'S FACES)

Take a couple of minutes and look around you at all the people you can see. God has created a beautiful rainbow of diverse people. The various skin shades range from pale white to dark black and everything in between. There are people of various heights and weights. And the range of hair colors and styles is almost endless. Yet in the midst of all this diversity, there is a commonality—each person has been made in the image of God. We are God's children. Look carefully at the faces of those with whom and to whom you are ministering. If you look deeply enough, can you see the image of God peeking through? Today, greet everyone you meet by saying, "I see Jesus in you!"

ACTION: *Walk around silently where you can walk past people and see their faces. Look at their face, smile, and breathe a prayer for them as you walk past. Then move to a place where you can sit and reflect on what you have seen.*

Scripture Reading Options

GENESIS 1:27

So God created man in his own image, in the image of God he created him; male and female he created them.

MARK 10:13-16

People were bringing little children to Jesus to have him touch them, but the disciples rebuked them. When Jesus saw this, he was indignant. He said to them, "Let the little children come to me, and do not hinder them, for the kingdom of God belongs to such as these. I tell you the truth, anyone who will not receive the kingdom of God like a little child will never enter it." And he took the children in his arms, put his hands on them and blessed them.

GO DEEPER—1 CORINTHIANS 12:13

Prayer Options

PRAYER OPTION 1:

Creator God, thank You for creating us in Your image. This is a great gift and not one that we take lightly. We have to confess that far too often, when we see others we don't consider that this person is also made in Your image. Instead, we sometimes see them as insignificant, unimportant, or just ignore them completely, which is perhaps the worst sin. Would You give us Your eyes so that we may always see others the way that You see them? Help us to treat everyone we encounter in the way You would treat them—with love, grace, and kindness. May this be so in our lives this week and for the future. Amen.

PRAYER OPTION 2:

Creative God, thank You for the incredible diversity we see around us. You have called us to minister in a world full of different, interesting people, each of whom is made in Your image. Even among Your servants there are many differences. As we share life with those we meet this week, may we be reminded that each one to whom we minister is Your beloved daughter or son and is, therefore, worthy of our full attention and love. Amen.

Key/Memory Verse

ROMANS 12:10

Be devoted to one another in brotherly love. Honor one another above yourselves.

 STATION 5—COMPASSION (HEART)

Has your heart ever really hurt for others? Have your ever felt like crying for someone and the injustice they are facing? If so, then you've experienced the beginning of compassion. However, feelings alone are not enough. Action is also needed. When you commit to serve, you've committed to follow through on compassionate feelings with action. Christians have a special reason to be compassionate—we reflect a God who is the very image of compassion. This is what motivates us to meet the needs of others.

ACTION: *Find a piece of paper (even a scrap will work) and walk to a solitary location. Draw a heart shape on the paper, or loosely tear its edges into the shape of a heart. Hold it and look at it for a moment. Now rip it in two. Consider how it feels to have your heart broken. Think for a moment of how many people around you feel "broken." Spend some time imagining how God feels for them. What does it mean to have a heart of compassion?*

Scripture Reading Options

ZECHARIAH 7:9

This is what the LORD Almighty says: "Administer true justice; show mercy and compassion to one another."

2 CORINTHIANS 1:3-4

Praise be to the God and Father of our Lord Jesus Christ, the Father of compassion and the God of all comfort, who comforts us in all our troubles, so that we can comfort those in any trouble with the comfort we ourselves have received from God.

GO DEEPER—MATTHEW 9:36-38

Prayer Options

PRAYER OPTION 1:

God, thank You for Your compassion. We recognize that we don't deserve it; we quickly turn from Your ways and fail to show compassion to others. Yet even when we withhold compassion, You offer it. When we fail to show mercy, You always give it. Would You enable us to always remember the compassion You have showed us—a compassion that seeks to understand us and point us to a better life. May Your example of compassion inspire us to be more compassionate to all with whom we come in contact. Amen.

PRAYER OPTION 2:

God of compassion, we know that You were compassionate to those You met. No matter how busy Jesus was, He would stop and give His presence, His touch, and His healing. He willingly elected to have His heart broken by the pain and misery of others when it would have been so much easier to stay away. Our prayer is that You would break our hearts this week through the people we encounter. May we see in every person we encounter a child of God; may we realize that as we minister to them we are also ministering to You. Amen.

Key/Memory Verse

MICAH 6:8

No, O people, the LORD has already told you what is good, and this is what he requires: to do what is right, to love mercy, and to walk humbly with your God. (NLT)

 ## STATION 6—TRUST (TRANSPORTATION)

Usually when we go on a mission trip or participate in service, it is necessary to use a vehicle of some sort to get there—a plane, van, car, or charter bus. Regardless of the mode of transportation, the fact is you had to have faith that the vehicle in which you traveled would in fact take you where you wanted to go. Furthermore, you had to trust the driver, knowing that she or he had your best interests in mind and wanted you to arrive at the end safe and sound.

ACTION: *Go to a place where you can sit near a parked vehicle or watch some sort of vehicle go by. If there is none, find a quiet place where you can focus on remembering your journey to this place. In your mind, begin to make the comparison between your physical journey and your spiritual journey. Reflect on where God has brought you thus far in your journey with Him. What have been the detours you've unexpectedly taken? Were there any speed bumps along the way (God's way of telling you to slow down)? And how well have you trusted the driver, God, to take you where He wants you to go?*

Scripture Reading Options

PSALM 20:6-7

Now I know that the LORD saves his anointed; he answers him from his holy heaven with the saving power of his right hand. Some trust in chariots and some in horses, but we trust in the name of the LORD our God.

PROVERBS 3:5-6

Trust in the LORD with all your heart and lean not on your own understanding; in all your ways acknowledge him, and he will make your paths straight.

GO DEEPER—ROMANS 15:13; JAMES 5:13-16

Prayer Options

PRAYER OPTION 1:

God, we know that Your Word tells us that You are trustworthy. And yet, when we are honest with ourselves, we don't believe it. If we did, we wouldn't try to do things in our power, nor would we forget to seek Your guidance for the next step of the journey. We are willing to trust ourselves to a driver every time we ride in a van or bus—in the same way, help us to place our trust in You to guide us in every facet of our lives. Remind us daily of Your incredible love for us as we seek to always follow You. Amen.

PRAYER OPTION 2:

Father God, Your actions have always been trustworthy. You've never failed to do what You said You would do, and even when we've turned our back on You, You've always remained faithful to us. As we journey together, gently remind us of the necessity of trusting You in all things so that we may truly enjoy life and become the people You've called us to be. Amen.

Key/Memory Verse

PSALM 37:5-6

Commit your way to the LORD; trust in him and he will do this: He will make your righteousness shine like the dawn, the justice of your cause like the noonday sun.

STATION 7—SERVANTHOOD (TOWEL)

Being a servant isn't always easy—sometimes it means we need to wash dirty, stinky feet. In the book of John, we find Jesus with a towel, doing just that. He takes a towel and uses it to dry the feet of His disciples after He's washed them. Jesus' example reminds us of our need to be a servant to those we encounter. Being a servant means giving to others for the sake of Christ. Not just on a mission trip or during a service project—those are the easy times to be a servant. Rather, how are you doing at practicing servanthood when no one is expecting it? How will you continue your servant ways after you return home?

ACTION: *Find a towel or a rag and pick it up. Look at it closely. Feel it. What does it remind you of? Is it clean or dirty? What has it been used for? When we answer the call to follow Jesus Christ, He hands us a towel and asks us to follow Him in His work, which is not always glamorous and famous. Consider how Christ is calling you to lay down your life to live as a servant.*

Scripture Reading Options

MARK 10:41-45

When the ten heard about this, they became indignant with James and John. Jesus called them together and said, "You know that those who are regarded as rulers of the Gentiles lord it over them, and their high officials exercise authority over them. Not so with you. Instead, whoever wants to become great among you must be your servant, and whoever wants to be first must be slave of all. For even the Son of Man did not come to be served, but to serve, and to give his life as a ransom for many."

GALATIANS 1:10

Am I now trying to win the approval of men, or of God? Or am I trying to please men? If I were still trying to please men, I would not be a servant of Christ.

GO DEEPER—JOHN 13:1-17; PHILIPPIANS 2:1-5

Prayer Options

PRAYER OPTION 1:

Gracious God, we have to acknowledge that being a servant isn't often fun. It's tough work and requires us to give up the things we want for the things others want. We confess to You our unwillingness to give of ourselves to others because we are too selfish. And yet, we know that being a servant isn't optional. Jesus himself calls us to do it. Therefore, we ask for Your strength to be a servant. Help us to not see servanthood as a drudgery, but rather give us the joy that can only come from serving others for Your sake. Amen.

PRAYER OPTION 2:

Incarnate Lord, You set for us the example we should follow by Your actions as You washed the disciples' feet. What seems to us as an unusual act was for You second nature; the action flowed out of who You are. We also desire that servanthood would not just be something we do but the very essence of who we are. We want to be Your servants, touching the world around us. Give us the courage to come not with power and might but with a basin and towel, and in so doing, may others see You at work through us and give You praise. Amen.

Key/Memory Verse

JOHN 13:14

Now that I, your Lord and Teacher, have washed your feet, you also should wash one another's feet.

 STATION 8—PERSPECTIVE (SHOES)

When you were a little kid, did you ever put on your mom's or dad's shoes and walk around the house? Most children do this because they want to be "grown up." In other words, they want to experience what it's like to be their mom or dad. When we get involved in service, we have the opportunity to put on the shoes of those we seek to serve. This is what Jesus did for us—He came to walk in our shoes and see life from our perspective.

ACTION: *Take a few minutes and look around you at the various shoes people are wearing. Think about the lives of the people who wear those shoes—where they've come from, what they do, where they're going. What would it be like to walk a mile in their shoes? What does life look like from their point of view? What are their hopes and fears? Only when we put ourselves into the "shoes" and lives of those to whom we minister will we ever really understand them and, therefore, help them draw closer to God.*

Scripture Reading Options

JOHN 1:14

The Word became flesh and blood, and moved into the neighborhood. We saw the glory with our own eyes, the one-of-a-kind glory, like Father, like Son, Generous inside and out, true from start to finish. (TM)

LEVITICUS 19:33-34

When an alien lives with you in your land, do not mistreat him. The alien living with you must be treated as one of your native-born. Love him as yourself, for you were aliens in Egypt. I am the LORD your God.

GO DEEPER—LUKE 24:13-35

Prayer Options

PRAYER OPTION 1:

Incarnate Lord, thank You for choosing to come and live among us. We recognize that You quite literally chose to become human so that You could understand what we go through. Your Word tells us that You were tempted in every way just as we are, and yet, You were without sin. It gives us the hope that if You could live sin-free, then so can we. And so we offer ourselves to You, as people who want desperately to follow You. We ask You to impart to us Your strength and wisdom as we endeavor to live in this world but not of it. Amen.

PRAYER OPTION 2:

God, we thank You for Your willingness to live among us through Your Son. Because You chose to step into our shoes, we know that we also should walk in the shoes of those we encounter. We don't always know what that experience will be like, but we know that because You walk with us, we don't have to be afraid. Grant that we may put ourselves in the shoes of others so that they may ultimately find You. Amen.

Key/Memory Verse

HEBREWS 4:15-16

For we do not have a high priest who is unable to sympathize with our weaknesses, but we have one who has been tempted in every way, just as we are—yet was without sin. Let us then approach the throne of grace with confidence, so that we may receive mercy and find grace to help us in our time of need.

section
two.
TRADITIONAL
MEDITATIONS

TRADITIONAL MEDITATION
TO LOVE AS
WE ARE LOVED

BY MATT WILL

(For Traditional Meditations, follow a designated prayer path, stopping at each station. If no path has been set up, choose different locations around you for each station.)

A surrendered soul will often cry out to God for a chance to love as we are loved. Have we ever truly allowed Him to speak His deep love to our soul? Our own service for Him often traps us; we try to show others His deep love, but we forget to be loved by God. We forget that the best way to love is to first be filled with His love.

Allowing ourselves to be loved is not as easy as we might first think. We have all had wounds inflicted upon us simply by living. Abuse, rejection, oppression, and violence have taught us false love. We have been loved for what we do. We are loved for our beauty, our athletic ability, our grades, or our positions. This sets a pattern and a cycle of living for an unreachable love.

There is hope. Although we face pain, bitterness, and brokenness, Christ's love can break through to reveal His love and to allow us to carry His love to others. This love allows you simply to be. Allow yourself to be loved as you begin this meditation. For some, the scriptures that you encounter on this journey will be like a glass of water in the desert. For others, you will have difficulty simply "being" and "receiving." You will find it difficult to drink the glass of water. Don't try to take the mystery out of God's love by trying to completely understand it. His love is to be experienced; let it be a mystery. Allow yourself to be still and know that the Creator of this world is the Lover of your soul. As you read this journey, feel free to skip, change, or remain at stations as long as you feel the Lord's leading.

STATION 1—HIS SCULPTING TOUCH ON YOUR LIFE

God is the master artist—we are His masterpiece. He has sculpted and crafted our very lives. Like a great artist, God is intimately involved in His work. He is as close to our lives as the potter's hands are to the clay.

ACTION: *Read this letter as if God wrote it directly to you. Allow the letter to speak its words to your heart.*
"Dear Beloved,

I know how you have longed for love. I have watched you seek it . . . And all the while I was waiting, always ready to wrap My arms around you and gather you to myself. My love for you began so long ago—way back when I formed you in your mother's womb. I loved you as a child. I've loved you through all your heartbreaks and disappointments and triumphs. I loved you even when you didn't love yourself, and when you didn't love Me. My love for you, unlike human love, is perfect; and I will continue to love you no matter what."[2] *Remember the times that you have longed for His love. Focus your mind on the truth that His hand is upon you—the Lord is near. Reflect on God's love and deep knowledge of you.*

Scripture Reading Options

JEREMIAH 1:5

Before I formed you in the womb I knew you, and before you were born I consecrated you; I have appointed you a prophet to the nations. (NASB)

GENESIS 1:1

In the beginning God created the heavens and the earth. (NASB)

ISAIAH 64:8

Yet, O LORD , you are our Father. We are the clay, you are the potter; we are all the work of your hand.

GO DEEPER—PSALM 139

---

2. Adapted from *Letters from God: God's Promises for You* (Franklin, Tennessee: Honor Books, 2000).

Prayer Options

PRAYER OPTION 1:

Dear Father, I thank You for creating me and for knowing that which You created. Words fail me, Lord, when I think of Your love, but I desire for You to know my gratitude. Please continue to fill me with the deep knowledge of Your love. I ask You to allow me to begin to know myself as You know me. Allow me to know Your deep love for me. Amen.

PRAYER OPTION 2:

(Choose one of the above scriptures and read it 4-5 times as your prayer. Read it slowly, prayerfully, and meditatively. Allow the words to seep into your soul as you pray them.)

Key/Memory Verse

PSALM 63:3

Because your love is better than life, my lips will glorify you.

 STATION 2—THE DEPTH OF HIS LOVE

Surely the suffering and death of Jesus provided a sign of deep love for His followers. His death for us was the ultimate sign of His love. Jesus was willing to endure anything to show how deeply He loved us. To know the love of Christ is to be changed. His words will leave an indelible mark upon our lives.

ACTION: *Think upon His wounds that bring healing to you. Meditate on the pain that Christ went through for you personally because of His deep love for you. Say again and again as part of your prayer, "by His wounds, I am healed."*

Scripture Reading Options

ISAIAH 53:4-5

Surely our griefs He Himself bore, and our sorrows He carried; yet we ourselves esteemed Him stricken, smitten of God, and afflicted. But He was pierced through for our transgressions, He was crushed for our iniquities; the chastening for our well-being fell upon Him, and by His scourging we are healed. (NASB)

MATTHEW 27:29-31

And after twisting together a crown of thorns, they put it on His head, and a reed in His right hand; and they knelt down before Him and mocked Him, saying, "Hail, King of the Jews!" They spat on Him, and took the reed and began to beat Him on the head. After they had mocked Him, they took the scarlet robe off Him and put His own garments back on Him, and led Him away to crucify Him. (NASB)

GO DEEPER—MATTHEW 27:35-42

Prayer Options

PRAYER OPTION 1:

Oh Lover of my soul, I long to get a glimpse of Your deep love for me. I desire to know Your love, but I fear that it will hurt to understand the depths of Your love. I fear if I truly see the mocking You went though for me, I will not be able to handle the feelings invoked in my soul. I fear the pain on Your face as You carried my afflictions will prove too great for me to handle. This leaves me wordless and motionless. All I can do is bow down before You. Amen.

PRAYER OPTION 2:

(As a prayer mediation, ask God to give you a fresh picture of how great His love truly is.)

Key/Memory Verse

EPHESIANS 3:16-19

I pray that out of his glorious riches he may strengthen you with power through his Spirit in your inner being, so that Christ may dwell in your hearts through faith. And I pray that you, being rooted and established in love, may have power, together with all the saints, to grasp how wide and long and high and deep is the love of Christ, and to know this love that surpasses knowledge— that you may be filled to the measure of all the fullness of God.

 ## STATION 3—GOD IS RICH IN MERCY

The truth of the matter is that if not for God's mercy we would be dead. If not for His kindness, we would be crushed by our sin and hopelessness. But God does not treat us as we deserve. He is rich in mercy. There is no shortage of it— God consistently rescues us, forgives us, lets us off the hook. He does not treat us as our sins deserve—all because of His loving mercy.

TRADITIONAL MEDITATION

ACTION: *Simply allow the Lord to speak to you as you read this scripture. Allow Him to lead you.*

Scripture Reading Options

EPHESIANS 2:4-7

But God, being rich in mercy, because of His great love with which He loved us, even when we were dead in our transgressions, made us alive together with Christ (by grace you have been saved), and raised us up with Him, and seated us with Him in the heavenly places in Christ Jesus, so that in the ages to come He might show the surpassing riches of His grace in kindness toward us in Christ Jesus. (NASB)

PSALM 13:5-6

But I have trusted in Your loving kindness; my heart shall rejoice in Your salvation. I will sing to the LORD, because He has dealt bountifully with me. (NASB)

GO DEEPER—PSALM 36:5-7; ROMANS 11:30-32

Prayer Options

PRAYER OPTION 1:

Lord, Your mercy is deep. You have drenched my life with Your overwhelming mercy. I now pray for You to help me to embrace the abundance of life that comes from Your love. Allow me to live in the light of Your love. Amen.

PRAYER OPTION 2:

(Reflect on God's kindness and what that has looked like in your life. See if you can think of two or three moments when you can point to God's mercy at work in your life. As a prayer, re-tell the story to God—what could have happened, should have happened, and what did happen because of His mercy. Give Him thanks for it. Then choose one of these scriptures and read it over three times as a part of your prayer.)

Key/Memory Verse

PSALM 100:5

For the LORD is good; His loving-kindness is everlasting and His faithfulness to all generations. (NASB)

STATION 4—IN HIM

We are in Christ and He is in us. Allow His love to live through you. Allow Him to speak words of love and truth to the depth of your soul. You can experience the love that comes from your truest lover if you begin to allow His life in you to shine through. His life in you can speak love to the wounded, broken, empty, and poor.

ACTION: *Reflect on what it means to abide in Christ and Christ in you. Ask Jesus to give you a visual illustration of His abiding power in your life.*

Scripture Reading Options

ACTS 17:28

For in Him we live and move and exist, as even some of your own poets have said, "For we also are His children." (NASB)

I JOHN 2:27

As for you, the anointing which you received from Him abides in you, and you have no need for anyone to teach you; but as His anointing teaches you about all things, and is true and is not a lie, and just as it has taught you, you abide in Him. (NASB)

GO DEEPER—JOHN 15:1-8

Prayer Options

PRAYER OPTION 1:

Lord, allow me to know You more. I thank You for allowing me to live in You—to have all my strength, hope, and breath come from You. I pray that You will help me begin to grasp the depths of Your love.

PRAYER OPTION 2:

(Ask Him to help your soul understand what it means to be in Him.)

Key/Memory Verse

JOHN 15:4

Abide in Me, and I in you. As the branch cannot bear fruit of itself unless it abides in the vine, so neither can you unless you abide in Me. (NASB)

STATION 5—KNOWING HIS LOVE ALLOWS US TO LOVE

It is one thing to know something by studying it—it is something else to know it by heart. When we experience the love of Christ, we are changed—His love enables us to love others. When we know how fully we are loved, it allows us to get past our own need—we no longer need or desire to use people to make us feel good about ourselves. When we are fully loved, we are set free to fully love others.

ACTION: *Read the following passages "formationally," not "for information." When we read for information, we read for content and knowledge—we read it scientifically. In formational reading, we allow the Lord to form and shape us through His Word. Read His Word for you and let the sound of it resonate in your soul. Pick out a particular phrase that emphasizes Christ's love, or the idea of being in Him. Try saying this phrase over and over as a prayer until it is all that you are thinking.*

Scripture Reading Options

EPHESIANS 2:8-10

For by grace you have been saved through faith; and that not of yourselves, it is the gift of God; not as a result of works, so that no one may boast. For we are His workmanship, created in Christ Jesus for good works, which God prepared beforehand so that we would walk in them. (NASB)

JOHN 13:34

A new command I give you: Love one another. As I have loved you, so you must love one another.

GO DEEPER—2 CORINTHIANS 5:17-20; LUKE 6:27-29

Prayer Options

PRAYER OPTION 1:

Lord, I thank You that You love who I am. Lord, this love that You show me allows me to become who I *really* am. I don't need to act like I am someone else. You allow me to *be* who I am. Help me to begin to understand what it means that You love me completely and that I am Your workmanship.

(Allow the Lord to center your mind on the thought that you are His beloved child, His workmanship, and His new creation.)

Key/Memory Verse

I JOHN 4:16, 19

We have come to know and have believed the love which God has for us. God is love, and the one who abides in love abides in God, and God abides in him . . . We love, because He first loved us. (NASB)

STATION 6—COMPLETE LOVE

The Bible says that God is love. His whole being, His essence, all that He does and is about is centered on love. God cannot help but love—it is His nature. When we say that God loves completely—we mean that He doesn't hold anything back. People can love partially—we can love someone and still act with selfishness. But not so with God. His very nature is love; He cannot do anything else but love. When God loves us, He loves us with His whole being, His entire self. Christ demonstrated this perfectly—there was nothing He kept for himself, not even His own life. He gave everything to show that there were no limits to His love.

ACTION: *Spend time pondering the words "complete love." Reflect on those things from your past that keep you from believing that God loves you completely. In your prayers, express to God that no matter what you have been through or have done—nothing from your past can change the nature of God. Take time to breathe the fullness of His love once again and ask God to help you experience abundant life.*

Scripture Reading Options

I JOHN 4:9-12

This is how God showed his love for us: God sent his only Son into the world so we might live through him. This is the kind of love we are talking about—not that we once upon a time loved God, but that he loved us and sent his Son as a sacrifice to clear away our sins and the damage they've done to our relationship with God. My dear, dear friends, if God loved us like this, we certainly ought to love each other. No one has seen God, ever. But if we love one another, God dwells deeply within us, and his love becomes complete in us—perfect love! (TM)

COLOSSIANS 2:2

That their hearts may be encouraged, having been knit together in love, and attaining to all the wealth that comes from the full assurance of understanding, resulting in a true knowledge of God's mystery, that is, Christ Himself. (NASB)

GO DEEPER—JEREMIAH 31:3-4; JOHN 10:10-18

Prayer Options

PRAYER OPTION 1:

Lord, Your complete love overwhelms me. How can You love me completely? How is Your love made complete in me? Thank You for Your complete work. Your perfect love shows me my value, my identity, my peace. Thank You for Your never-failing, everlasting, "without condition" love. Amen.

PRAYER OPTION 2:

(Cup your empty hands together, palms up. Repeat this prayer until you can accept it by faith: "I receive Your love today, O Lord.")

Key/Memory Verse

PSALM 145:8-9

The LORD is gracious and merciful; slow to anger and great in loving-kindness. The LORD is good to all, and His mercies are over all His works. (NASB)

 ## STATION 7—RELY ON THE RELIABLE: GOD IS LOVE

God is love. Allow that message to sink deep within you. Allow it to go past all of your hurts and misconceptions. Allow the truth of His love to speak to you.

ACTION: *Spend time meditating on the phrase: "God is love." Wait in silence for several moments, allowing God the opportunity to speak to you.*

Scripture Reading Options

1 JOHN 4:16

We have come to know and have believed the love which God has for us. God is love, and the one who abides in love abides in God, and God abides in him. (NASB)

sacred space

PSALM 86:15

But you, O Lord, are a compassionate and gracious God, slow to anger, abounding in love and faithfulness.

DEUTERONOMY 7:9

Know therefore that the LORD your God, He is God, the faithful God, who keeps His covenant and His loving-kindness to a thousandth generation with those who love Him and keep His commandments. (NASB)

GO DEEPER—HOSEA 11:8-11, 14:1-4

Prayer Options

PRAYER OPTION 1:

Lord, Your nature is love. I thank You for enfolding me in this deep love. I pray that as I become more formed into Your likeness, more of my being becomes love. Allow me to love as You love. Allow me to become part of Your love. Let my hands and my feet become instruments of Your deep love. Amen.

PRAYER OPTION 2:

Dear God, search my heart. Fill me with Your Holy Spirit and examine the shadows of myself. Show Your light on every part of my heart—and in Your mercy change anything in me that doesn't reflect Your love. Amen.

Key/Memory Verse

1 JOHN 2:24

Let that abide in you which you heard from the beginning. If what you have heard from the beginning abides in you, you also will abide in the Son and in the Father. (NASB)

 ## STATION 8—UNVEILED

The Lord pours His love into us and begins to shine on us and through us. As the love of God abides in us, we become full of His light and His glory. God makes us reflections of Him in this world. His love and His glory allow us to live free.

ACTION: *Ask God to remove any barriers between Him and you. Pray that His love would flow through you to those near you and to the world. Pray that the veil would be removed that keeps others from seeing Him in you.*

Scripture Reading Options

2 CORINTHIANS 3:18

But we all, with unveiled face, beholding as in a mirror the glory of the Lord, are being transformed into the same image from glory to glory, just as from the Lord, the Spirit. (NASB)

MATTHEW 5:16

Let your light shine before men in such a way that they may see your good works, and glorify your Father who is in heaven. (NASB)

GO DEEPER—EXODUS 33:18-23

Prayer Options

PRAYER OPTION 1:

Jesus, transform me into Your likeness. Transform my hate into love. Transform the dark parts into light. Transform all of me to reflect Your glory. Lord, I thank You that I am not left to change my own heart. Thank You, Lord, for transforming me to reflect Your glory. Allow all of me to reflect Your love. May I reflect You. Amen.

PRAYER OPTION 2:

(Focus your mind on this phrase, "Reflect the Lord's glory." Allow the Lord to speak to you through this.)

Key/Memory Verse

PSALM 80:3

O God, restore us and cause Your face to shine upon us, and we will be saved. (NASB)

 ## STATION 9—TO LOVE THE UNLOVABLE LIKE OURSELVES

Imagine that Jesus has written you the following note:
"There will always be those people in this world who seem somewhat unlovable . . . But be thankful for them. For they are like an invitation for you to come to Me and to allow Me to love through you. When someone is good and kind and easy to love, you don't need My help. But when someone is cantankerous and moody, it requires more than you—it requires Me. And when you involve Me, we begin to

make a difference. My love combined with your love is a miracle waiting to happen."[3]

ACTION: *Silently picture the face of someone who is "unlovable." Pray for them. Ask for God's mercy that you might see them differently. Listen as the Lord leads you to ideas of how to love those in your life that seem unlovable.*

Scripture Reading Options

MATTHEW 5:3

Blessed are the poor in spirit, for theirs is the kingdom of heaven. (NASB)

MATTHEW 5:44

But I say to you, love your enemies and pray for those who persecute you. (NASB)

GO DEEPER—MATT 5:38-41; MARK 1:40-41

Prayer Options

PRAYER OPTION 1:

Lord, help me to love those who at times seem unlovable. Allow them to feel that I love them completely with love that comes from You. Allow me to get past all that stops me from loving them. As I go through my days, help me to reflect the hope that You have given me. Lord, guide me to those who rarely feel love from others; give me the power to embrace them with the love that has captured my heart. Amen.

PRAYER OPTION 2:

(Repeat several times) Lord Jesus, have mercy on me. Fill my heart with compassion and pure love.

Key/Memory Verse

LUKE 4:18

The Spirit of the Lord is upon me, because He anointed me to preach the gospel to the poor. He has sent me to proclaim release to the captives, and recovery of sight to the blind, to set free those who are oppressed. (NASB)

---

3. Adapted from *Letters from God: God's Promises for You* (Franklin, Tennessee: Honor Books, 2000).

STATION 10—IF I HAVE NOT LOVE I HAVE NOTHING

Love makes the difference between an act of kindness and an act of selfishness. Without love, our actions are full of mixed motives—in the absense of love, we don't have the best interest of the other person in mind. Without love, we may do something nice for someone, but we may be using them or expecting something in return. But love expects nothing in return—it just gives. Love makes all the difference.

ACTION: *Allow the Lord to examine your heart. Ask God to write His love on your heart. Ask Him to infuse love into all of your actions.*

Scripture Reading Options

I CORINTHIANS 13:1-3

If I speak with the tongues of men and of angels, but do not have love, I have become a noisy gong or a clanging cymbal. If I have the gift of prophecy, and know all mysteries and all knowledge; and if I have all faith, so as to remove mountains, but do not have love, I am nothing. And if I give all my possessions to feed the poor, and if I surrender my body to be burned, but do not have love, it profits me nothing. (NASB)

JOHN 13:34-35

A new commandment I give to you, that you love one another, even as I have loved you, that you also love one another. By this all men will know that you are My disciples, if you have love for one another. (NASB)

GO DEEPER—ISAIAH 61:1-3

Prayer Options

PRAYER OPTION 1:

Lord, my prayer is that You would restore my heart and speak Your love to me. I pray that I would now be used to restore hope and love to those who need it. Allow me to speak hope to the poor. Help me to bring freedom to the imprisoned. Allow me, Lord, to love others in a way that brings freedom to their hearts. Aid me to love others in a way that allows them to truly be themselves. Amen.

PRAYER OPTION 2:

Lord Jesus, please pour out the Holy Spirit upon me to increase the depth of my love and compassion for others. Give me new eyes that I may see those around me in a new way—that I may see them the way You see them. And grant me the grace to pour out my life the way that You did for me. Amen.

Key/Memory Verse

ROMANS 13:8

Let no debt remain outstanding, except the continuing debt to love one another, for he who loves his fellowman has fulfilled the law.

 STATION 11—UNQUENCHABLE THIRST

All that we do comes from the gift of love that the Lord has given us. As we embrace His love, we are filled with a desire to know Him more. This is our unquenchable thirst—it is our thirst for Him. As we seek His face, our lives begin to mirror His love. We take what the Lord has done in our hearts and turn it outward. Our thirst for Him becomes our passion to serve—because we begin to love what He loves. Our lives become like His—lives given in service for others. As we thirst for God, we thirst to live for Him.

ACTION: *Read one or two of these scriptures over and over several times. As you read them, ask the Lord to allow a word or phrase to stand out and speak to your heart. When you have that phrase, focus on it and allow the Lord to speak to you through it.*

Scripture Reading Options

PSALM 42:1-2

As the deer pants for the water brooks, so my soul pants for You, O God. My soul thirsts for God, for the living God; when shall I come and appear before God? (NASB)

PSALM 22:26

The afflicted will eat and be satisfied; those who seek Him will praise the LORD. Let your heart live forever! (NASB)

GO DEEPER—I CORINTHIANS 13:4-8

Prayer Options

PRAYER OPTION 1:

Thank You Lord for Your deep gift of love. Your love is the transforming power in me that changes me even when I am unaware of it. Lord, as the famished look for food and as the thirsty look for water, I search for You. I need Your transforming power in my life. Amen.

PRAYER OPTION 2:

Dear Lord, don't leave me as I am. Make me like You. Make my love like Yours. Let my life count for something—let me know Your will, what You are doing in this world—and let me become Your hands and feet. My life is Yours. Amen.

Key/Memory Verse

PROVERBS 8:17

I love those who love me; and those who diligently seek me will find me. (NASB)

STATION 12—THANK THE LORD FOR THE PRIVILEGE OF BEING HIS SERVANT AND VESSEL

God has enough power that He doesn't need us to help Him do His will. He chooses to call us to join Him—to participate in His love. It is His joy that we become a part of His love for the world.

ACTION: *Ask the Lord which verse He would have you mediate on as you go through your day. Take a moment to journal all that God is showing you. Write out a prayer of thanksgiving to Him.*

Scripture Reading Options

JEREMIAH 1:5

Before I formed you in the womb I knew you, and before you were born I consecrated you; I have appointed you a prophet to the nations. (NASB)

PSALM 63:3

Because Your loving kindness is better than life, My lips will praise You. (NASB)

sacred space

Prayer Options

PRAYER OPTION 1:

(Repeat several times) Lord, I thank You that Your love is better than life. Help me to live reflecting Your love.

PRAYER OPTION 2:

Prayer of St. Francis

"Lord, make me an instrument of thy peace. Where there is hatred, let me sow love; where there is injury, pardon; where there is doubt, faith; where there is despair, hope; where there is darkness, light; where there is sadness, joy. O divine Master, grant that I may not so much seek to be consoled, as to console; not so much to be understood as to understand; not so much to be loved as to love; for it is in giving that we receive; it is in pardoning that we are pardoned; it is in dying that we are awakened to eternal life."[4]

Key/Memory Verse

MATTHEW 22:37-39

And He said to him, "You shall love the Lord your God with all your heart, and with all your soul, and with all your mind." *This is the great and foremost commandment. The second is like it,* "You shall love your neighbor as yourself." (NASB)

---

4. Don Postema, *Space for God* (Grand Rapids, Michigan: Faith Alive Christian Resources, 1997).

TRADITIONAL MEDITATION
CENTERING ON THE TRUTH

BY MATT WILL

(For Traditional Meditations, follow a designated prayer path, stopping at each station. If no path has been set up, choose different locations around you for each station.)

The ability to center our minds and lives on truth is a valuable skill in a world full of spin and lies. Everywhere we turn, lies seem to bombard us. If we are not careful we begin to build a foundation of fear and false values rather than a foundation built on Christ. We fear ourselves—who we are. We wonder if we have any worth at all. The only protection against these fears is to center on truth. The lies of the world block our hearts from living in the truth of His life in us. We can spend months living under different lies that speak to our own fears. We experience fears and feelings of low self-worth because we do not focus on the truth of who we are in Christ. Instead we build our identities out of other things. We start to become what the world tells us we should be. The world's values and sense of worth are unstable ground to stand on. These other identities fail us every time.

There is a firm place to stand. Part of the journey to get there involves centering on the truth that we find in the Scripture. This is often the truth of our identity, of who God calls us to be. It is in focusing on the truth that we begin to find the freedom that we seek. It is not through a simple formula, a good sermon, or a great meditation that we find freedom; rather, the Spirit of the Lord speaks freedom and identity to our hearts. Allow Him at this time to speak those things to your heart. As Moses was changed by his encounter with the Lord, you can be changed from believing the lies in your life to believing the truth that God speaks to us.

99

This journey will help you look at the Scripture. As you use it, allow the Spirit to speak God's truth to the lies you may believe regarding your worth, lies that war against your soul. When you hear truth from the Spirit, you will begin to experience freedom, as the Lord speaks through His Word to your heart. As you read, be open to hear the Lord reveal to you the lies that your heart believes. Do not simply look into your own heart to see what failures are there that you may perceive; instead ask the Holy Spirit to teach you what areas He would like to transform in your life today. Transformation is a process; if we look at every area of weakness, we tend to feel overwhelmed with guilt and condemnation. Instead, ask God to reveal areas to you where you need to hear His truth. Remember to discern the difference between conviction and condemnation. Conviction is when you hear the inner voice of God's Spirit speaking to you about circumstances for which you might need to ask forgiveness, or for ways to change your behavior. Condemnation, which is not from the Lord, is when you hear or feel things like "you are a bad person" or "you are worthless." Condemnation is a lie about your identity. Conviction is a truth from the Spirit. As you begin this path, be on guard against condemnation and be open to conviction. Condemnation enslaves you. Conviction brings about ultimate freedom.

Special Stations for Centering on Truth

Whereas many meditations have different stations at which to stop and ponder, this meditation gives the journeyer freedom to stop when he or she feels led. There are four simple stations. They are designed for walking toward a central location and then moving out away from it again. Follow the directions and move as you feel led at each point. If you feel your heart and mind wandering, look back to the area where you feel you should focus and recenter on the truth that God has shown you. This meditation is written as if you are moving through a prayer path. To use it in another setting, simply pick a location to be the central point of your meditation journey—perhaps a scenic location at a park or a hilltop. Moving toward the "central" area is station 1, entering into the "center" space and waiting there is station 2, leaving that spot and starting your return is station 3, and journeying back to the "regular" world is station 4.

STATION I: THE JOURNEY BEGINS (ENTERING THE PATH)

As we begin to center on truth, we walk as if taking a journey away from the world and its lies; we move to draw closer to God in order to hear His truth. We strip away all distraction and shed all other voices so we may clearly hear God speak truth to our lives.

ACTION: *Practice the following as you walk between stations. As you start walking, begin to center in and allow the Lord to clear your thoughts. Allow the Lord to take away all the distractions from your day. As you walk between stations, try not to talk to the Lord, rather, be quiet with Him. Try as much as possible to simply be still before Him. If it helps to focus your thoughts, try to focus on a word as you walk. Try focusing on the word by repeating it in your mind or saying it to yourself as you walk to the center of the prayer path, or whatever location you have chosen for your "center" station. If your mind begins to wander, recenter on the word that you felt led to focus on. Fix your entire being on the Lord. This will help to bring about settledness within your soul.*

This is a list of words that you can use to center your thoughts. Feel free to use these words or any others that reflect a truth about God or His relationship to you:

Peace	Mercy	Healer	Loving
Love	Joy	Comforter	Savior
God's Love	Patience	Father	King
Trust	Kindness	Strong	Jesus
Help	Spirit	Protector	Helper
Truth	Life	Vine	Friend
Justice	Faithfulness	Potter	Reverence
Wounded Healer	Guide	Patient	Compassionate
Good	Creator	True	Merciful
Awesome	Freedom Giver	Silent	Just
Holy	Righteous	Beautiful	Consistent
Nurturing	Wise	Generous	Sovereign
Leader	Powerful	Kind	

Scripture Reading Options

PSALM 46:10

Be still, and know that I am God; I will be exalted among the nations, I will be exalted in the earth.

PSALM 100:3

Know that the LORD is God. It is he who made us, and we are his.

Prayer Options

PRAYER OPTION I:

Holy Spirit, as I walk today I pray that You will help me center myself in Your presence. I release to You everything that holds me back from Your presence. Help me to be still in this place. Make all the distractions in my heart go away. Lord, I need Your power to grant me peace. Amen.

PRAYER OPTION 2:

(Repeat several times)
Lord Jesus Christ, Son of God, have mercy on me, a sinner.

 ## STATION 2: RECEIVING THE TRUTH (ENTERING THE CENTER)

(Read this as you enter the center of the path, or whatever location you have chosen. Practice the exercise as you wait there.)

We often believe lies about who we are and our own worth. These lies seem to sneak up on us. As you enter the center station, ask the Lord to begin to reveal to you a lie that you have believed about your identity.

ACTION: *Ask the Lord to give you a truth from Scripture that He would have you center on as you sit before Him. Prayerfully look at the list of scriptures below or search your Bible. Ask the Lord to reveal a scripture that speaks truth to your soul. Spend some time waiting before the Lord. Find a comfortable position and take your time. If distractions come into your mind, pray about them, release them to the Lord, look back to the truth the Lord is revealing, and continue on your journey.*

Centering on Truth Scripture Reading Options

JOHN 1:12

Yet to all who received him, to those who believed in his name, he gave the right to become children of God.

ROMANS 5:1

Therefore, since we have been justified through faith, we have peace with God through our Lord Jesus Christ.

I JOHN 1:9

If we confess our sins, he is faithful and just and will forgive us our sins and purify us from all unrighteousness.

ROMANS 8:1

Therefore, there is now no condemnation for those who are in Christ Jesus.

ROMANS 8:28

And we know that in all things God works for the good of those who love him, who have been called according to his purpose.

PHILIPPIANS 1:6

Being confident of this, that he who began a good work in you will carry it on to completion until the day of Christ Jesus.

PHILIPPIANS 3:20

But our citizenship is in heaven. And we eagerly await a Savior from there, the Lord Jesus Christ.

I CORINTHIANS 3:16

Don't you know that you yourselves are God's temple and that God's Spirit lives in you?

PHILIPPIANS 4:13

I can do everything through him who gives me strength.

JEREMIAH 1:5

Before I formed you in the womb I knew you, before you were born I set you apart.

GO DEEPER—ROMANS 8:37-39; I CORINTHIANS 6:17, 19; I JOHN 5:18; ACTS 1:8; EPHESIANS 2:10; 2 CORINTHIANS 5:17; 2 TIMOTHY 1:7; HEBREWS 4:16; JOHN 15:15

Prayer Options

PRAYER OPTION 1:

Holy Spirit, reveal to me a lie that I believe about my identity. Or please simply reveal to me a deep need that You would like to fill right now. I will wait and listen. Amen.

PRAYER OPTION 2:

Holy Spirit, reveal to me the truth as I look over the scriptures and listen to You. (Look at the list of scriptures for this station.)

 ## STATION 3: LIVING IN THE TRUTH (LEAVING THE CENTER)

(Read this as you begin to exit the center of the path, or whatever location you have chosen for this station. Practice this as you ready yourself to leave this space.)

As we hear and receive the truth of God's Word, we must determine to live in that truth. It does not do any good to hear the truth and then turn away from it. We must continue in it and live it. We hear the truth, and we walk in the truth.

ACTION: *As you ready yourself for the return journey, continue to ponder the truth that the Lord has spoken to you. In the same way that you focused in on a word when you began, focus in on the truth as you start your return. Say the truth over and over again until it becomes a part of your being.*

Scripture Reading Options

JOHN 8:32

Then you will know the truth, and the truth will set you free.

GALATIANS 5:13

You, my brothers, were called to be free. But do not use your freedom to indulge the sinful nature; rather, serve one another in love.

GO DEEPER—PSALM 15:1-5

Prayer Options

PRAYER OPTION 1:

Lord, thank You for speaking Your truth to me. I thank You for allowing me to know You. I pray that the truth that You have spoken to me will be placed deep within my heart. Lord, allow me to know the truth in my heart and not just in my head. Amen.

PRAYER OPTION 2:

Lord Jesus, Your Word is truth. Bind Your truth to my heart and life. Give me the strength to walk in Your truth all my days. Let Your Holy Spirit bring Your truth to my mind and my life every day. Amen.

Key/Memory Verse

GALATIANS 5:25

Since we live by the Spirit, let us keep in step with the Spirit.

 ## STATION 4: THE JOURNEY OUT INTO THE WORLD (EXITING THE PATH)

(Read and reflect on these questions as you exit the center.) As you move to the end of this meditation, prepare your heart to take the truth you have received back into your world. You will once again be surrounded with the lies of this world, and many competing voices will clamor for your attention. Take this part of the meditation journey to prepare yourself to face them by holding to the truth God has given you. Don't forget what the Lord has spoken to you. Walk in the light of His truth.

ACTION: *As you complete the journey, reflect on what the Lord has spoken to you. Ask yourself questions such as these: Lord, is there any way You are asking me to live differently in response to what You have taught me? Lord, is there anything else You would like to speak to me through this experience? Lord, what is a creative way that I can remember the truth that You spoke to me today?*

Scripture Reading Options

PROVERBS 4:25-27

Let your eyes look directly ahead and let your gaze be fixed straight in front of you. Watch the path of your feet and all your ways will be established. Do not turn to the right nor to the left; turn your foot from evil. (NASB)

Prayer Options

PRAYER OPTION 1:

Lord, never let me forget the truth of who I am in You. I am Your child. Remind me as often as I need it that Your truth lives in me and I need not fear. I thank You for setting my feet on the solid rock of Your truth. Amen.

PRAYER OPTION 2:

Father God, I stand strong in Your Word. My desire is to walk with You in Your truth. I renounce the lies of the devil; I reject the lies of this world. I am a child of the King and a citizen of heaven. As I live in this world, protect me from believing the world's lies and fill me with Your love for those around me. Amen.

Key/Memory Verse

(Review or memorize the verse that stood out to you as you walked this path. Go back to it often to recenter on its truth.)

TRADITIONAL MEDITATION
WALK TO THE CROSS

BY MATT WILL

(For Traditional Meditations, follow a designated prayer path, stopping at each station. If no path has been set up, choose different locations around you for each station.)

In our world today we have trouble grasping the reality of the shame surrounding the path to the Cross. We have unintentionally glamorized Christ's sacrifice. The current symbol has no meaning that is comparable to what we find in the gospels. A cross is seen as something that we adorn ourselves with rather than as a tool of brutal destruction. The struggle as we begin this meditation journey is in reconstructing the devastation of the Cross. As we begin this journey, we pray that the Lord will give us a picture of the reality of the Cross. This was the most shameful, dehumanizing experience that humanity has created to destroy a life. If we catch this reality we will be changed.

As you ponder the Cross, be open to change. The Lord will use the scriptures in this meditation to transform your heart. Do not merely read these scriptures; allow the scriptures to read you. To meditate on Christ's journey to the Cross is one of the most powerful exercises an individual can allow the Lord to do in them. Allow the great power of the Lord to reorient your understanding of the Cross.

 ## STATION I—THE LORD HAS SET YOU APART
Open yourself to what the Lord is doing in your life. Quiet yourself and ask the Lord to guide your steps and thoughts. Feel free at any time during this meditation to sit, lie down, or stand as you pray.

ACTION: *Invite the Lord to begin in you a deep realization of His love for you which was reflected through His life.*

Scripture Reading Options

PSALM 4:3-4

You can be sure of this: The LORD has set apart the godly for himself. The LORD will answer when I call to him. Don't sin by letting anger gain control over you. Think about it overnight and remain silent. (NLT)

PSALM 62:1-2

I wait quietly before God, for my salvation comes from him. He alone is my rock and my salvation, my fortress where I will never be shaken. (NLT)

GO DEEPER—REVELATION 1:6

Prayer Options

PRAYER OPTION 1:

Jesus, as I begin this journey to the Cross, I see that I must sit before You to be transformed. When I rest before You, my heart is healed. Lord, allow me to join You on this journey to the Cross. Reorient all that needs reorientation in my soul. I wait for You.

PRAYER OPTION 2:

(Read one of the above "Scripture Reading Options" and meditate on it. Ask the Lord to give you a word or phrase within the scripture upon which to center your attention and quiet your soul.)

Key/Memory Verse

MATTHEW 11:28

Then Jesus said, "Come to me, all of you who are weary and carry heavy burdens, and I will give you rest." (NLT)

STATION 2—PROPHECY

Before the world's formation, Christ was. His coming was prophesied by the prophets of old. We join in the story of His coming. Ask the Lord to allow you to grasp the gift of His prophecy.

ACTION: *Ask the Lord to allow you to grasp the enormity of the prophesy of Christ to come, His appearance on earth, and His future return. (Give yourself time to let this idea sink in.) Choose one of these passages from the "Scripture Reading Options" and read it over three times.*

Scripture Reading Options

ISAIAH 53:4-5

Yet it was our weaknesses he carried; it was our sorrows that weighed him down. And we thought his troubles were a punishment from God for his own sins! But he was wounded and crushed for our sins. He was beaten that we might have peace. He was whipped, and we were healed! (NLT)

MARK 1:2-3

Following to the letter the scroll of the prophet Isaiah.
Watch closely: I'm sending my preacher ahead of you; He'll make the road smooth for you. Thunder in the desert! Prepare for God's arrival! Make the road smooth and straight! (TM)

GO DEEPER—JOHN 1:1-9; MARK 1:1-8; ISAIAH 7:14;

Prayer Options

PRAYER OPTION 1:

Jesus, Your coming and life had been prophesied throughout human history. I thank You for inviting me to join in this great story that You have created. I sit in awe of the fact that the story of Your coming was prophesied thousands of years prior to Your arrival in the flesh. Lord, help me to see the entire story. Help me to see You pulling me toward yourself.

PRAYER OPTION 2:

(Numerous prophecies point to Christ's coming as the pivotal point in history. Take a few moments to meditate on the sovereignty of God throughout history. He has been and always will be in charge.)

Key/Memory Verse

MALACHI 3:1

"Look! I am sending my messenger, and he will prepare the way before me. Then the Lord you are seeking will suddenly come to his Temple. The messenger

*of the covenant, whom you look for so eagerly, is surely coming," says the LORD
Almighty.* (NLT)

 ## STATION 3—MINISTRY

When Jesus was on earth, He brought freedom and life to
the hurting. He spoke of the Kingdom. He healed, cast out
demons, and gave power to others to do likewise.

ACTION: *Try to enter into one of the stories from the "Scripture
Reading Options." Imagine yourself as a disciple or simply an onlooker.
What are some emotions that you have? What are your thoughts, fears,
joys, and hopes? Choose one of the following scripture passages to
prayerfully consider.*

Scripture Reading Options

MATTHEW 14:14

*A vast crowd was there as he stepped from the boat, and he had compassion
on them and healed their sick.* (NLT)

MARK 5:1-13

*So they arrived at the other side of the lake, in the land of the Gerasenes.
Just as Jesus was climbing from the boat, a man possessed by an evil spirit ran
out from a cemetery to meet him. This man lived among the tombs and could
not be restrained, even with a chain. Whenever he was put into chains and
shackles—as he often was—he snapped the chains from his wrists and smashed
the shackles. No one was strong enough to control him. All day long and
throughout the night, he would wander among the tombs and in the hills,
screaming and hitting himself with stones.*

*When Jesus was still some distance away, the man saw him. He ran to meet Je-
sus and fell down before him. He gave a terrible scream, shrieking, "Why are you
bothering me, Jesus, Son of the Most High God? For God's sake, don't torture me!"
For Jesus had already said to the spirit, "Come out of the man, you evil spirit."*

Then Jesus asked, "What is your name?"

*And the spirit replied, "Legion, because there are many of us here inside this
man." Then the spirits begged him again and again not to send them to some
distant place. There happened to be a large herd of pigs feeding on the hillside
nearby. "Send us into those pigs," the evil spirits begged. Jesus gave them permission. So the evil spirits came out of the man and entered the pigs, and the entire*

herd of two thousand pigs plunged down the steep hillside into the lake, where they drowned. (NLT)

GO DEEPER—MATTHEW 14:14-21; JOHN 11:28-44

Prayer Options

PRAYER OPTION 1:

Jesus, I thank You for Your love and ability to heal. I pray that I can begin to live in light of Your ministry. Lord, I pray for Your continued transforming of my heart into a mirror of Your heart.

PRAYER OPTION 2:

(Meditate on the Lord's desire and ability to minister to you now and ask Him to meet your areas of need. Many scriptures show Christ as Healer, Savior, Sanctifier, and Coming King. Ask Him to meet you where you are, and then sit and receive from the Lord.)

Key/Memory Verse

ACTS 2:22

People of Israel, listen! God publicly endorsed Jesus of Nazareth by doing wonderful miracles, wonders, and signs through him, as you well know. (NLT)

 STATION 4—RECEIVE HIS TRUTH

Allow this to be a time when you sit before the Lord and hear His truth speak to you. Reflect on the fact of His prophesied coming and His ministry. Allow Him to speak to you.

ACTION: *Ask the Lord to reveal to you where you do not believe His truth in your life. Listen for the Lord to reveal your need to your heart. Listen for the Lord to reveal His truth in your heart.*

Scripture Reading Options

JOHN 16:13

When the Spirit of truth comes, he will guide you into all truth. He will not be presenting his own ideas; he will be telling you what he has heard. He will tell you about the future. (NLT)

GALATIANS 5:1

So Christ has really set us free. Now make sure that you stay free, and don't get tied up again in slavery to the law. (NLT)

sacred space

Prayer Options

PRAYER OPTION 1:

Lord, Your love amazes me. I pray that Your truth guides me. Guide me through Your revelation. O Spirit of truth, speak to my heart.

PRAYER OPTION 2:

Lord I pray that You would replace the lies that I believe with Your truth and freedom. Reveal to me Your truth. I don't want to live by lies. I want to walk in Your truth. Speak Your truth to me, and I will walk in it. Amen.

Key/Memory Verse

PSALM 100:5

For GOD is sheer beauty, all-generous in love, loyal always and ever. (TM)

 ## STATION 5—SERVANTHOOD

Christ lived a life of service. He fed the poor and ministered to the hurting. He called for all to be righteous. He took up a servant's role—He took up a towel and cleaned the dirty feet of the disciples. He declared that if you cannot allow Him to clean you, then you have no place in His Kingdom.

As you read this passage, allow yourself to enter into the story. Imagine yourself there. Picture Christ cleaning your feet.

ACTION: *Spend time resting in the realization that Jesus humbled himself to take the place of a servant for you. Ask the Lord what your response to His act of service to you should be.*

Scripture Reading Options

JOHN 13:3-5

Jesus knew that the Father had put him in complete charge of everything, that he came from God and was on his way back to God. So he got up from the supper table, set aside his robe, and put on an apron. Then he poured water into a basin and began to wash the feet of the disciples, drying them with his apron. (TM)

JEREMIAH 33:8

I'll scrub them clean from the dirt they've done against me. I'll forgive everything they've done wrong, forgive all their rebellions. (TM)

GO DEEPER—PSALM 51:2-7; JOHN 13:3-17

Prayer Options

PRAYER OPTION 1:

Lord, how could You, the maker of the universe, become the servant of all? Lord, how could You wash me? How could You humble yourself to die on a cross for me? How could You take such a position? O Jesus, thank You for Your cleansing. Allow me to grasp what it means that the maker of heaven and earth has taken up the basin and the towel and a place on the Cross.

PRAYER OPTION 2:

(Read John 13:3-10 and imagine you are there. He is King of all, yet He wants to serve you. He even says "Unless I wash you, you have no part with me." Spend time meditating on your God who wants to serve you. He wants to show you His love. Ask Him to give you a visual picture of His love, or a phrase that will help you grasp it.)

Key/Memory Verse

MARK 9:35

He sat down and summoned the Twelve. "So you want first place? Then take the last place. Be the servant of all." (TM)

 ## STATION 6—TAKE THIS CUP

On Jesus' journey to the Cross He released all that He had to the Father. He grieved deeply. He eventually came to a place where He released His very life. It was in the garden that He reconciled the sacrifice within himself. Being betrayed by one that He loved, He began to move toward that which He knew He must do.

ACTION: *Read one or more of the "Scripture Reading Option" passages, and simply ask Jesus how He would have you respond to the scriptures you read.*

Scripture Reading Options

MARK 14:32-36

And they came to an olive grove called Gethsemane, and Jesus said, "Sit here while I go and pray." He took Peter, James, and John with him, and he began to be filled with horror and deep distress. He told them, "My soul is crushed with grief to the point of death. Stay here and watch with me."

He went on a little farther and fell face down on the ground. He prayed that, if it were possible, the awful hour awaiting him might pass him by. "Abba, Father," he said, "everything is possible for you. Please take this cup of suffering away from me. Yet I want your will, not mine." (NLT)

ROMANS 8:15

This resurrection life you received from God is not a timid, grave-tending life. It's adventurously expectant, greeting God with a childlike "What's next, Papa?" (TM)

GO DEEPER—MARK 14:32-46

Prayer Options

PRAYER OPTION 1:

Jesus, I can't imagine the pain of betrayal that You must have gone through. Surely You could have stopped it all with one word. I thank You for holding on through the struggle of Gethsemane—Your struggle brought me life when You laid Your life down. Lord, this journey is overwhelming and hard for me to understand. Please further my understanding as I continue on this journey. Allow me to understand what it means that the cup You drank from was also set out for the disciples to drink from as well. Lord, do I need to drink that cup also? Show me Your will.

PRAYER OPTION 2:

(Read Mark 14:32-46 and try to imagine the pain of release your Savior went through. Allow the Holy Spirit to use your imagination to speak to you. Allow this picture to take root in your soul.)

Key/Memory Verse

MARK 14:36

"Abba, Father," he said, "everything is possible for you. Please take this cup of suffering away from me. Yet I want your will, not mine." (NLT)

STATION 7—JESUS MOCKED

After the betrayal in the garden, the Lord made His way to Jerusalem. He was mocked, beaten, and scourged for our sins. He went through overwhelming pain until His death. His closest friends claimed they did not know Him.

ACTION: *Reflect on the love that Jesus has for you. Allow the pain and the suffering that comes from this story to sink into your mind and heart.*

Scripture Reading Options

MARK 15:16-20

The soldiers took him into their headquarters and called out the entire battalion. They dressed him in a purple robe and made a crown of long, sharp thorns and put it on his head. Then they saluted, yelling, "Hail! King of the Jews!" And they beat him on the head with a stick, spit on him, and dropped to their knees in mock worship. When they were finally tired of mocking him, they took off the purple robe and put his own clothes on him again. Then they led him away to be crucified. (NLT)

ISAIAH 52:14

Many were amazed when they saw him—beaten and bloodied, so disfigured one would scarcely know he was a person. (NLT)

GO DEEPER—MATTHEW 27:35-44

Prayer Options

PRAYER OPTION 1:

Lord, the shame and pain You endured is so unknown to me. You went through overwhelming torture and mocking for me. I cannot comprehend the suffering You faced. Lord, as I picture the blood drip from the crown of thorns, I find that I feel so unworthy of this love. I just want to say thank You for what You went through. I know there is no way my actions will ever repay Your sacrifice, but I pray that in some way I might remain faithful to the sacrifice You gave for me.

PRAYER OPTION 2:

(Reread one of the passages from the "Scripture Reading Options" for this station. Focus on one word or phrase, one detail from the story, and repeat that word or phrase several times as your prayer. Let that one detail help you capture the reality of the sacrifice of Christ that you may praise Him.)

Key/Memory Verse

ISAIAH 50:6

I followed orders, stood there and took it while they beat me, held steady while they pulled out my beard, didn't dodge their insults, faced them as they spit in my face. (TM)

 ## STATION 8—YOU BECOME THE RIGHTEOUSNESS OF GOD

Christ endured pain for you, so that through His pain you might gain life and righteousness.

ACTION: *Focus in on the word "righteous." Continue to think on this word until it is all you are thinking about. Read one of the passages from the "Scripture Reading Options" over again several times. Ask the Holy Spirit what it means to be "righteous."*

Scripture Reading Options

2 CORINTHIANS 5:21

For God made Christ, who never sinned, to be the offering for our sin, so that we could be made right with God through Christ. (NLT)

I PETER 2:24-25

He personally carried away our sins in his own body on the cross so we can be dead to sin and live for what is right. You have been healed by his wounds! Once you were wandering like lost sheep. But now you have turned to your Shepherd, the Guardian of your souls. (NLT)

GO DEEPER—ROMANS 6:8-11, 17

Prayer Options

PRAYER OPTION I:

(Stop for a moment and tell the Lord your feelings about what He went through on your behalf. Thank the Lord for His sacrifice for you.)

PRAYER OPTION 2:

Lord, allow me to understand what it means that I "become the righteousness of God." Help me to understand what the word "righteousness" means. Please help me to understand what this means, and more than that, help me to walk in it. Amen.

Key/Memory Verse

GALATIANS 3:13

Christ redeemed us from that self-defeating, cursed life by absorbing it completely into himself. Do you remember the Scripture that says, "Cursed is everyone who hangs on a tree"? That is what happened when Jesus was nailed to the Cross: He became a curse, and at the same time dissolved the curse. (TM)

 ## STATION 9—DEATH ON THE CROSS "IT IS FINISHED"

After the betrayal, mockery, and journey to Calvary, Christ hung on the Cross until His death. He died to bring about healing in our hearts. He died to bring us freedom from sin.

ACTION: *As you read the story of His death, imagine that you are there. Imagine what it looks like. Try to prayerfully put yourself there. Then repeat to yourself the phrase, "It is finished," several times. Ask the Lord to show you all that is meant by that declaration of Jesus from the Cross.*

Scripture Reading Options

JOHN 19:30

When he had received the drink, Jesus said, "It is finished." With that, he bowed his head and gave up his spirit.

JOHN 15:13

And here is how to measure it—the greatest love is shown when people lay down their lives for their friends. (NLT)

GO DEEPER—MARK 15:33-38; PHILIPPIANS 2:5-8

Prayer Options

PRAYER OPTION 1:

(Christ died on the Cross. He experienced enormous pain. Allow your soul to enter this story and spend time mourning His death as one would grieve the death of a friend.)

PRAYER OPTION 2:

Lord, thank You for Your death on the Cross. I will never truly understand the agony You experienced within Your spirit. Lord, as I reflect on Your death it brings humbleness and a feeling of awe. Words fail my thanksgiving. I can only say that I love You, Jesus.

Key/Memory Verse

JOHN 15:13

And here is how to measure it—the greatest love is shown when people lay down their lives for their friends. (NLT)

STATION 10: RESURRECTION

After Christ's death on the Cross, He fulfilled the prophecy and rose to life again. Rejoice! He has destroyed the power of death for our life. We do not serve a God that is dead; rather, we serve a God who is alive.

ACTION: *Prayerfully reflect on what it means for you that Christ died and then was brought back to life, conquering death.*

Scripture Reading Options

MATTHEW 28:2-6

Suddenly there was a great earthquake, because an angel of the Lord came down from heaven and rolled aside the stone and sat on it. His face shone like lightning, and his clothing was as white as snow. The guards shook with fear when they saw him, and they fell into a dead faint.

Then the angel spoke to the women. "Don't be afraid!" he said. "I know you are looking for Jesus, who was crucified. He isn't here! He has been raised from the dead, just as he said would happen. Come, see where his body was lying." (NLT)

ACTS 4:10-12

Let me clearly state to you and to all the people of Israel that he was healed in the name and power of Jesus Christ from Nazareth, the man you crucified, but whom God raised from the dead. For Jesus is the one referred to in the Scriptures, where it says, "The stone that you builders rejected has now become the cornerstone." There is salvation in no one else! There is no other name in all of heaven for people to call on to save them. (NLT)

Go Deeper—Mark 16:9-15

Prayer Options

Prayer Option 1:

Jesus, thank You for Your work. I accept Your life in me. I pray that I may live in the light of Your work. I pray that the Cross will no longer be merely a symbol. Thank You.

Prayer Option 2:

Lord, to die such a brutal death and be raised to life in such a glorious way is truly amazing. I praise You for Your power. I praise You for Your submission, and now victory over death itself. Lord, I need You to help me grasp what it means that You have triumphed over death. It is just too big of an idea, and we live at a time when we see death around us—and it seems so powerful and final. Speak to my heart the truth of Your victory. Amen.

Key/Memory Verse

Matthew 28:6

He isn't here! He has been raised from the dead, just as he said would happen. Come, see where his body was lying." (NLT)

STATION 11—HIS PASSION CALLS FOR CHANGE IN YOU

His death brought about healing for you. You have walked through His Passion; take time now to ask what areas of your life He would have you begin to change. Ask Him to heal any areas He reveals to you. Seek after healing and "resurrection" for the "dead" areas of your life that need His touch.

 ACTION: *Pray as you feel led.*

Scripture Reading Options

1 Thessalonians 5:23-24

Now may the God of peace make you holy in every way, and may your whole spirit and soul and body be kept blameless until that day when our Lord Jesus Christ comes again. God, who calls you, is faithful; he will do this. (NLT)

TITUS 3:5-7

He saved us, not because of the good things we did, but because of his mercy. He washed away our sins and gave us a new life through the Holy Spirit. He generously poured out the Spirit upon us because of what Jesus Christ our Savior did. He declared us not guilty because of his great kindness. And now we know that we will inherit eternal life. (NLT)

GO DEEPER—ROMANS 12:2; LUKE 14:25-35

Prayer Options

PRAYER OPTION 1:

Lord, thank You for the work You did for me. Your pain was unimaginable. Thank You for allowing me to go on this journey of knowing You more. I never want to live disconnected from the reality of Your Cross. Keep me in the awe of understanding how to respond to Your deep love. Keep me mourning when it is time to mourn and rejoicing when it is time to rejoice.

PRAYER OPTION 2:

Lord, reveal to me what areas need healing. Lord, I give You (<u>whatever He revealed to you</u>). Bring about Your transformation. Replace (<u>what He revealed to you</u>) with the reality of Your life and Your love.

Key/Memory Verse

COLOSSIANS 1:10

Then the way you live will always honor and please the Lord, and you will continually do good, kind things for others. All the while, you will learn to know God better and better. (NLT)

 ## STATION 12—HIS RETURN

We are now left with a promise. We are left with the promise that the Lord dwells within us and that He will return for us to take us to be where He is. Deep joy is derived from the fact that Jesus is coming back. His return will bring about His perfect kingdom.

ACTION: *Spend time reflecting on the scriptures below and spend some time in worship of the living Christ, giving thanks to God that your name is written in the book of life.*

Scripture Reading Options

HEBREWS 9:28

So also Christ died only once as a sacrifice to take away the sins of many people. He will come again but not to deal with our sins again. This time he will bring salvation to all those who are eagerly waiting for him. (NLT)

REVELATION 22:20

He who testifies to these things says, "Yes, I am coming quickly." Amen. Come, Lord Jesus. (NASB)

GO DEEPER—REVELATION 21:1, 3-5

Prayer Options

PRAYER OPTION 1:

Lord, I join the many that have gone before me in gratefully awaiting Your return. It is beyond my comprehension to know what it will be like on that day. I wait for You like children waiting for their father to come home from work. I am standing at the door, listening for the sound of Your arrival! I join with the many who have gone before me in saying, "Come, Lord Jesus."

PRAYER OPTION 2:

(Spend time praising the Lord for His love for you. Give thanks to Him that He is returning to bring about His kingdom.)

Key/Memory Verse

REVELATION 22:20

He who testifies to these things says, "Yes, I am coming quickly." Amen. Come, Lord Jesus. (NASB)

USING A PRAYER PATH (PRAYER LABYRINTH)

This section is written for those who would like to use a prayer path for their meditations, or facilitate prayer journey exercises for groups at your campus, church, or home. You can of course use "Meditations for Common Places," which are designed for a specific location—the mall, the park, a mission trip, etc. However, if you want to use the traditional meditations and follow the ancient tradition of walking a path, this chapter will get you started with preparations.

When most people begin to look at the prayer labyrinth, they find its mazelike appearance confusing. It looks like you could get lost in the midst of the circuits. However, even though the prayer journey looks like a maze, it is not a maze. While a maze might have walls and dead ends, a labyrinth is laid out on the ground and has no dead ends. If you want to understand what I mean, look at the diagram of the labyrinth on the next page. Trace it with your finger. There are no dead ends or wrong turns. This demonstrates the simplicity of taking the prayer journey.

Note that the "Traditional Meditations" found in this book can be used in just about any location—simply designate 8-12 stations (in your home, church, or anywhere outdoors) and do one meditation step at each spot. (You could of course do all the steps in one spot, but there is a beauty in moving from one location to another—it provides a new perspective. Moving from one place to another also mirrors the idea of being on a journey, which is a good way to look at spiritual disciplines and life as a whole.)

Meditating at stations along a path is an ancient tradition. There are several cathedrals that have a prayer path mapped out on the floor in mosaic tiles. For information on how to create a prayer path or prayer labyrinth, you can search the Internet, or download free step-by-step setup directions and facilitator's guidelines from www.barefootministries.com! Here is what a typical path looks like:

The walkway of this path is designed to be two feet wide, so the total diameter is 32 feet across. You can mark off this pattern on a floor with masking tape, or create it in an outdoor setting with rocks or sticks. Place station numbers at appropriate places as in the dia-

sacred space

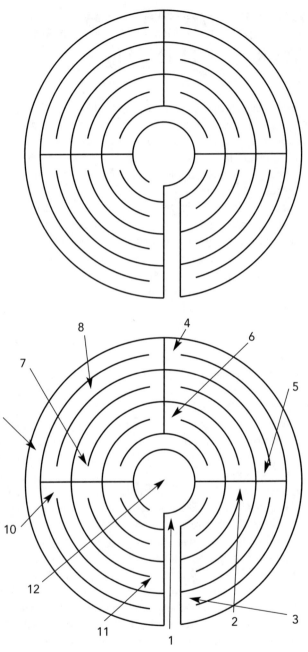

gram. (Make sure they are spaced apart from each other so that several people can use the path at the same time without disturbing each other.)

If you don't want to or do not have space for a traditional labyrinth, there are many other options for preparing a space for your meditations. Two simple options are setting up stations in a room without the labyrinth or moving your stations outdoors.

Room Setup

If you have space constraints, or do not wish to set up a prayer labyrinth, you can use a simple room set up for station meditations. Simply take station numbers and set them around the room in a logical, flowing manner. Make sure that you have plenty of room for meditating in each of the places where you set up the different stations. If you have a number of rooms, (for example, in a church that has Sunday School rooms), you might want to consider making each room a different mediation point with different visual tools or mediation helps. Make sure you use arrows to point the way to the next station. Work to create an atmosphere at each station with visual elements, and even sounds and smells. Make all the stations appropriate for the meditation. Allow the visual objects to speak to the journeyer as much as the written meditations do.

Outdoor Setup

Another great place to use is the outdoors. You can set up stations according to "Meditation for the Outdoors" included in this book, or just set up enough stations for a traditional meditation of your choice. Allow the outdoor setting to set the atmosphere for your stations.

The main physical tool that you will need to set up a meditation room or outdoor path is station numbers and arrows. Set the numbers and arrows in obvious locations. One of the main jobs of setting up the exercise is to minimize the distractions. A clearly directed path helps the participants connect with God easily as they walk on the journey.

Atmosphere

After choosing how you want to set up your meditation space, you will need to prepare the atmosphere. Atmosphere plays a large part in helping to set people free from distractions so they can focus on God. One of the main jobs of the facilitator is maintaining the atmosphere. There are many different ways to create and maintain a good atmosphere. Whether you build a labyrinth or place station numbers in a room or outdoor path, you will need to make sure the atmosphere encourages meditation. Setting the atmosphere for a room could entail an entire transformation of the room to make it useable as a place for meditation. An authentic worship experience will be aided by an atmosphere that removes distracting elements and adds elements that set a worshipful mood, look, and feel.

Here are some helpful ideas for setting a worshipful, meditative atmosphere:

- Set the right lighting with candles or luminaries. (Lighting is an important part of creating a meditative atmosphere.) Use enough lighting to read the meditation, but not too much to distract.
- Use background music to cover noise distraction. (Soft worshipful or instrumental music is best—sometimes it is good to combine with live worship.)
- Use visual tools when appropriate. (For example: When doing the garden of Gethsemane station from "Walk to the Cross," you might want to set up a garden. For the story of the woman caught in adultery, use sand and rocks. To illustrate the temptation of the rich young ruler, use a plate full of coins).
- Prepare communion or foot washing at one of the stations.
- Use plants to transform a sterile room and add color.
- Provide journals and Bibles at appropriate places.

Path Guidelines

After you have the area set up, the next thing to consider is how to lead a group through the experience. When doing a labyrinth, it is important to understand that there is a lot of freedom, but there are also guidelines so journeyers do not distract each other from what may be happening inwardly. Here are some useful guidelines when facilitating the labyrinth. You can post these on a sign by the entrance to the path.

1. Turn off all pagers and cell phones.
2. Walk the circuits as they are laid out before you. (You might need to explain how to walk the circuits at this point. Help them see it is not a maze where they can choose a dead end or get lost. There is no wrong turn in a prayer path labyrinth.)

3. Stop at the different stations and practice the corresponding meditation.
4. Stay as long or as short as you like at a station.
5. If the person in front of you on the path is taking longer than you, feel free to pass them.
6. Feel free to stand, lie down, or sit as you pray.
7. Please maintain the silence to help facilitate the prayerful atmosphere.
8. Give others permission to spend time with God and not be a distraction to you.

Personal Devotions

The meditations in this book can also be used apart from any meditation room or path. They are designed for use in your everyday life, in common places. Meditation is just one way to draw closer to God—it is not just something that happens in special times. Meditation can happen all throughout your day. It is easy to figure out ways to creatively integrate meditation into your entire day.

- Meditate on one station a day. Take 8-12 days to go through a meditation.
- Meditate briefly on all the stations each day. Do this for a week, allowing the flow and the story of the meditation to penetrate your soul.
- Take little moments throughout your day when you are free and recenter on the truths of the meditation. For example, return to a brief time of reflection and prayer between meetings or classes.
- Spread the stations throughout your day. Do a few stations in the morning, a few in the afternoon, and a few in the evening.
- Journal as you work through the stations. Write down what you hear the Lord speaking to you.
- In a small group, write your own meditations and trade them with other members of your group for devotions during the week.